DIGITIZING YOUR COMMUNITY'S HISTORY

D0881968

**Recent Titles in Libraries Unlimited's
Innovative Librarian's Guide Series**

Digitizing Audiovisual and Nonprint Materials:
The Innovative Librarian's Guide
Scott Piepenburg

Making the Most of Digital Collections through Training and Outreach:
The Innovative Librarian's Guide
Nicholas Tanzi

DIGITIZING YOUR COMMUNITY'S HISTORY

The Innovative Librarian's Guide

Alex Hoffman

INNOVATIVE LIBRARIAN'S GUIDE

LIBRARIES
UNLIMITED™

An Imprint of ABC-CLIO, LLC

Santa Barbara, California • Denver, Colorado

Copyright © 2016 by Alex Hoffman

All rights reserved. No part of this publication may be reproduced, stored in a retrieval system, or transmitted, in any form or by any means, electronic, mechanical, photocopying, recording, or otherwise, except for the inclusion of brief quotations in a review, without prior permission in writing from the publisher.

Library of Congress Cataloging-in-Publication Data

Names: Hoffman, Alex, 1986– author.
Title: Digitizing your community's history : the innovative librarian's guide / Alex Hoffman.
Description: Santa Barbara, CA : Libraries Unlimited, 2016. | Series: Innovative librarian's guide | Includes bibliographical references and index.
Identifiers: LCCN 2015050728 (print) | LCCN 2016017068 (ebook) | ISBN 9781440842405 (paperback) | ISBN 9781440842412 (ebook)
Subjects: LCSH: Libraries and community. | Local history materials—Digitization. | Public services (Libraries) | BISAC: LANGUAGE ARTS & DISCIPLINES / Library & Information Science / Collection Development.
Classification: LCC Z716.4 .H64 2016 (print) | LCC Z716.4 (ebook) | DDC 025.2—dc23
LC record available at https://lccn.loc.gov/2015050728

ISBN: 978-1-4408-4240-5
EISBN: 978-1-4408-4241-2

20 19 18 17 16   1 2 3 4 5

This book is also available as an eBook.
Visit www.abc-clio.com for details.

Libraries Unlimited
An Imprint of ABC-CLIO, LLC

ABC-CLIO, LLC
130 Cremona Drive, P.O. Box 1911
Santa Barbara, California 93116-1911
www.abc-clio.com

This book is printed on acid-free paper ∞

Manufactured in the United States of America

Contents

Introduction

We all have stories. These are the stories we live, the stories we tell ourselves, and the stories we are a part of with those around us. Aside from the narratives in our head, we have physical artifacts that represent the stories we have lived. Photographs, letters, video, and sound are all remnants of the journeys we have made, or made by those before us.

Without the objects and documents that help pass on the stories, we lose something central to humanity. This is one of the great things about the digital era we live in. Being so connected allows us to bond over shared experiences, histories, and events.

We all know that libraries have been shifting and changing over the past decade. Once thought of as repositories for books and other information, libraries are now thriving community centers, still full of books, stories, and wisdom, but also cultural programs, access to new tools, and opportunities for education. Particularly, many libraries now offer the ability for patrons to learn new technologies like digitization.

Digitization offers patrons the opportunity to get in touch with their own personal and historical materials, their memories, and their own life narratives. What previously required extremely cost-prohibitive equipment and knowledge only a small group possessed is now very accessible, with high-quality results and a shallow enough learning curve that even those who have never touched a computer can learn.

What this book offers is a high-level view of what it takes to start a DIY digitization program at your library. From garnering the support of your institution to learning the equipment and engaging the community in these historical materials.

Specifically, this book will cover what digitization is and why it is important, how to begin planning out your services, what equipment and software to consider, storage and archiving options, developing ways to engage the community, and training staff and the public on the process.

Since this book focuses on getting the general public to digitize their materials, we are going to take an approach that should fit the average person. This takes into consideration time constraints, beginner levels of knowledge, and sustainable and practical expectations and practices. We want to help people preserve their materials, but in a way that suits their lifestyle and their comfort level. We will not be digitizing things for the Library of Congress here, but family materials that we want to preserve for our children and grandchildren.

This book is about digitization, and using this process to share the stories we have, to connect with one another, with the library as the common thread in our communities.

From small rooms with a single scanner to larger labs supported by classes and programs, there is a digitization program that can fit within any library's means. Let us dive in.

Chapter 1

The Basics

WHAT IS DIGITIZATION?

Simply put, digitization is the process of converting information into a digital format. You can think of it as taking physical, real-world objects, or analog media (photos, vinyl records, video tapes) and transporting them to the modern, technological realm of computers, the web, and mobile devices.

With so much of our work centered within the digital world, it is not only convenient to have digitized versions of our materials, but it is also important for storing and preserving, creating redundant copies of our materials, and of course, sharing with others.

Digitization provides us with ways to connect with our history on new and varied levels. We can conveniently and quickly access digital versions, work to correct any flaws, such as tears, discoloration and missing pieces, as well as work with the materials in various forms of new media with minimal risk of damaging the original.

History

The first real digitization project began in 1971 with Project Gutenberg. The first document to be digitized was the U.S. Declaration of Independence, at the University of Illinois. The project's aim was to create electronic texts of influential and classical literature and documents.

Throughout the 1970s and 1980s, there were a number of other projects, including Thesaurus Linguae Graecae, the Oxford Text Archive, and the ARTFL Project, that were all early efforts to digitize important texts (Johnston, 2012).

Many other universities and organizations started projects to preserve literature and the humanities well into the 1990s. These were all efforts by large institutions to preserve important historical and humanitarian documents.

What came next is what I refer to as mass digitization, which is what this book aims to be a part of. As technology became smaller and more affordable, institutions took on larger and larger digitization projects, and amateurs and hobbyists were able to begin their own digitization projects at home.

For the past 20 years, many people have had the chance to begin digitizing their materials with greater ease, security, and convenience. Many of us have had scanners and other tools for digitization in our homes for nearly two decades, possibly without realizing it. It is this accessibility that has made DIY digitization such a viable method of preserving our past.

Where We Are Now

At this point, there is much equipment that is accessible and easy to use. Scanners are affordable and relatively user-friendly, and interfaces for converting video and audio signals from analog to digital are as well. The information needed to begin digitizing can be found in numerous books and websites. Because of this, it is a great time to be working on any digitization project, whether for your own personal fulfillment, or for a larger local history or genealogy project.

Digitization has also been around long enough for those with experience to offer helpful insights that will make the experience more enjoyable and meaningful to anyone who embarks on one of these projects.

Many libraries have developed digital media labs and makerspaces, often equipped with scanners and other digitization equipment. Many homes have printers and scanners, and a large number of us have smartphones. These tools are all readily available and affordable, making digitization a very accessible process to engage with today.

Future Trends

While it may seem that most materials are able to be digitized, there are improvements around the corner. Some of the most recent changes come with three dimensional (3D) printing and scanning. Libraries around the country have been setting up makerspaces with these printers and scanners, enabling residents to get their hands dirty with models, prototypes, and other fun objects. While the focus has been on 3D printing, 3D scanning will prove to be an exciting advancement for digitization.

3D scanning will allow us to digitize 3D objects, not just the traditional media. We can now capture the shape, size, and texture of important artifacts, whether it is family jewelry that has been passed down for generations, or a piece of local history that is important to the community.

While still in its infancy, especially at the consumer level, we can look forward to improvements such as higher-scanning resolutions, resulting in more accurate models and reproductions, and more advanced materials beyond the plastics that most library's 3D printers use today.

Other advances will be in storage. More reliable and long-lasting technologies will offer more peace of mind. As search algorithms improve, we will also be able to better manage large collections of digitized materials.

Digitization versus Digital Preservation

It is important to note the difference between *digitization* and *digital preservation,* since the terms are often interchanged.

Digitization is simply the process of converting analog materials into a digital format. Once they have been digitized, the digitization process is over. What you do with the resulting files is much more important.

Digital preservation is the planning and actions one takes to keep the files and materials intact over the long term. This includes your backup strategies, storage of the files, and anything else that goes into keeping the files safe and whole.

WHY DIGITIZE?

Contributed by Michael Mulholland

It is a part of human culture to remember the past. Future generations will want to know about your community and the part it played in the bigger picture of American history. Your patrons ask library staff what can they do with those old newspapers, books, photographs, and documents that have been lying around for decades in their trunks, attics, basements, and garages?

All those items contain the history of the people that lived in your community. They are the documentation of all the events that make your community unique. Any preservation of records done now will be accessible to future generations. Simply stated, you are preserving history! They will know about the first settlers and immigrants who came from all parts of the world to start your community.

The local public library is the prime location for saving all that history. Historically, libraries have always been repositories of books that dealt with all fields of knowledge. As technology advanced, libraries started offering phonograph records, then cassettes, and now Blu-ray, streaming devices, and eBooks. Libraries started keeping local newspapers on microfilm so that customers could research the past. If there was no historical society in the community, people began to donate their own books, private collections, even artifacts to the local library because the library seemed the logical place to keep that knowledge. However, libraries may not have the physical storage space or archival capabilities to preserve those items. Technology, however, has reached a point to preserve local history in various electronic formats.

What makes your place unique? The geographic location and size of your community will have an influence on its history. A small New England town founded in the early 1700s is quite different from a fast-growing industrial city in the Midwest. Who were the original European colonizers of your area? The French in Louisiana, the Spanish in Arizona, and the Russians in Alaska will certainly have left their marks. Even the very first settlers, the Native American tribes, will also have a part in your community's local history.

So then, what makes your community unique?

- The name of your community
- The street names
- The old factory that made or still makes saddles, rocking chairs . . . whatever it was!
- The gigantic oak tree on Main Street
- The deserted gas station off the highway
- The vintage car owned by Mr. Johnson

Did some historical event take place in your community? Was a famous person born in your community? Was something invented or first made in your community?

Preserving History

The most obvious and arguably the most important reason for digitizing our materials is to preserve our history. This is central to the whole process. By preserving the past, we can connect with it, and most importantly, learn from it.

Just as we study history throughout our schooling to glean insights from the past, we can do the same from our personal and local histories. Not just the history we have personally lived, but the history of those who have made us, have raised us, have set up roots, and have informed the cultures and practices we were raised in. Whether we have accepted or rejected them, learning about our past tells us about why we are who we are, where we came from, and possibly, where we are going.

Seeing the slow passage of time also helps us to appreciate where we are. Browsing through old photos and documents, we can see how technology has changed, and how people lived before the conveniences and power of our current technology.

We can witness lifestyles that are no longer around, or lifestyles that have evolved to what they are today. We can witness how historical events have shaped the world, how they affected our families, and their influence on our lives today. This all helps us to see how our little piece of life fits into the larger puzzle.

Even greater than that, connecting with our past may help us see the things we all hold in common. By seeing these common threads, we can connect better with those around us today.

With the importance of these materials, it is critical to create backups and copies. Creating duplicates in their same physical format is expensive, time consuming, and sometimes requires specialized knowledge and training. Making digital copies has a shallower learning curve, is more cost effective, and makes better use of your time.

It should be noted that while digitization is important, it is not a panacea for the woes of real-world materials. As some may have experienced, computers and other technologies fail us, hard drives crash, and files are lost. Despite this, it is still important to digitize.

The key to digitization is redundancy. Spread out over many different storage mediums, such as hard drives, flash drives, and cloud storage, digitization provides an extra layer of protection for the materials that mean so much to us.

Convenience

Having digital copies of your materials can be much more convenient in terms of sharing, distribution, access, and organization. A digital copy of your films can be quickly shared with friends and relatives across the world. Even for your own viewing pleasure, these files are rarely more than a few clicks away.

Further Study and Corrections

Building off of convenience, having digital copies allows us the flexibility and opportunity to study our materials even further. Having the ability to quickly pull up a file, magnify it, make changes, or use other tools provides us with more insights and connection into our history. Even consumer-level programs, like the new Photos for Mac OS X, use facial recognition software to tag the same person in multiple photos, adding another level of information to our photos. The digital world offers new levels of interaction, information, and engagement.

Lastly, a digital version allows you to further connect with the work by fixing any flaws, such as scratches, dust, or color issues, by editing, or further enhancing the work, in a technical or artistic way. Digital copies offer great flexibility that you will not find in the source material, as well as the ability to make mistakes without damaging the original. The software and hardware available makes it possible to restore photos, audio, and video that may have otherwise been lost to the stresses of the physical world.

WHO IS IT FOR?

Digitization is for *everyone*. While nothing can replace the tangible nature and charm of our photos, letters, and other personal artifacts, creating digital copies of our materials is valuable to anyone looking to preserve them and explore their past.

With changes in technology and tools, as well as simplification in software and better user experiences, digitization is something that can be engaged in, no matter your technical skill. Those comfortable with computers or any form of media production will likely find themselves quick to adopt the process, and those with little to no technical knowledge, with a little patience and a willingness to learn, will be able to comfortably sink into the process.

Individual Benefits

Individually, digitization allows one to learn new and relevant skills pertaining to technology and other related fields. The skills one learns when going through digitization will stay with him or her for some time. The extra skills may even come in handy when looking for employment or for tackling new projects and opportunities in the workplace.

Project Management

Digitization projects can be large and complex. Learning to organize, process, and plan projects like these are easily translatable into any sort of professional environment. You will learn the organizational skills necessary to sift through large amounts of materials and data. On top of that, you will learn to make effective decisions regarding what is important, what can be left out, what to focus the most resources on, and how to properly curate your collection. This can be done objectively, or with a more, if a collection is to tell a particular story or narrative.

These projects also involve time management, especially if you are dividing up digitization time out among several days or months, depending on the size of the project. Accounting for troubleshooting, equipment downtime, and other roadblocks, will prove to be a valuable skill. These are all necessary for any job, or life in general.

Tech Skills

The terminology, tasks, and other processes needed for a successful digitization project provide a solid foundation of tech skills necessary for any job today. Especially in libraries, we understand that there are many people who still lack the basic skills needed to operate a computer. Learning to digitize will teach people the basics of computing, such as files, folders, and file formats (for photos, audio, videos and documents). They will also learn to troubleshoot the equipment and problem solve basics errors and issues.

Those who take their projects to the next level will learn more advanced skills like photo, audio, and video editing and restoration. This is a broad area that involves many tech skills, like learning more about file formats, the details, characteristics, and possibilities of digital media. These all quickly branch out into more advanced forms of tech knowledge, such as hardware knowledge revolving around scanners, cameras, conversion equipment, and so forth.

Diving into editing can also lead to more creative skills, such as design, compositing, and other advanced media creation skills. Working with digitized materials in this way may also inspire someone artistically. The possibilities of taking old photos, video or audio, and doing something new, interesting and creative are vast. Digitization does not have to be as straightforward as preserving photos. The projects can go in any direction, and it is that freedom that leads to learning new skills and coming up with new ideas.

Communication Skills

We all know how important communication skills are, not only in the workplace, but in life in general. Working through the digitization process, especially if for a specific storytelling or history project, will help people hone their communication and storytelling skills. Getting in touch with our personal and family histories only enhances our worldview, our perspectives, and ultimately, our ability to better communicate with others. Telling stories effectively and communicating clearly are skills that are invaluable within any line of work.

Community Benefits

On a larger scale, digitization helps tighten the threads that bind a community together. What better way to learn about your neighbor than by sharing in their history, their memories, and their cultural stories.

It is no secret that a mutual understanding and respect of varying cultures and histories is a pillar of strong, peaceful, and vibrant communities. Digitization gives us all an opportunity to connect with ourselves and with each other.

Library Benefits

Libraries want to be part of the fabric of the community, and digitization is another way they can be a part of that. Positive, meaningful experiences are what will draw people into our buildings and to our programs, and offering the ability to connect with one's past and share in others is a great way to do that. By offering residents opportunities for connection and for learning new skills, we ensure our place in their hearts and lives.

MAKING IT UNDERSTANDABLE AND ENJOYABLE

The importance of making the digitization process approachable, simple, and enjoyable cannot be overstated. This may seem easy, but it is definitely a challenge. The process may be quick to pick up for those who are familiar with technology, but can instill pause, and even fear in those who are new to it.

Technology has allowed us to do wonderful things, but if you cannot make it a relevant, valuable, and a somewhat human experience, it will only end up turning people off to technology and the opportunities it offers them. For many in your community, this may be their first time, or at least a formative experience for them using new tools. We need to make sure it is a positive one!

Keeping it simple does not mean dumbing down the process, or simply reducing steps. It means boiling down the elements of digitization to a succinct and understandable set of steps that help the patron achieve his or her digitization goals. Simple is difficult to achieve, but it is crucial to a positive experience.

Make the Process Meaningful

Making it enjoyable, and relieving any technology-related fears the user may have makes all the difference. For example, I was working with an older woman in a one-on-one appointment. She told me she would like to scan a large collection of family photos, but was in no particular rush.

It began as most of my one-on-ones do. We sat down in the library's digital media lab, and I prefaced her on the scanning process, as well as asked her about what she hoped to do. After a few minutes, we began to scan the photos, and I noticed that she began to cry. It turns out, she had been wanting to digitize these photos for years, but was so afraid of the process that she never got around to it. She was so relieved at the ease of the process and that someone had taken the time to sit down with her and walk through it step by step.

By simply taking the time to work with our patron, listen to her needs, and allay any fears she had, we were able to help someone digitize her treasured personal photos, and help her get through her tech-related phobias. She associates that positive experience with the library as a whole and has been back several times to continue scanning her photos.

Set Expectations

While we will do our best to provide a simple, meaningful digitization experience for all of our patrons, there will inevitably be issues to overcome. We should plan for them, embrace them, and use them as learning experiences.

It is important to set this expectation from the get-go, especially with patrons who are inexperienced with technology. Let them know that if an obscure error pops up while they are scanning, it is part of the process, and an opportunity for them to learn technology troubleshooting (which is just part of using any digital equipment). By prefacing them on the nature of the process, these hurdles, which could easily lead to frustration, we can give them the tools to wade through the roadblocks and keep the process meaningful and enjoyable.

Offer Assistance and Community

One of the most important aspects of offering digitization capabilities is to offer the support that many in the community will seek out with their projects. Simply providing guides or instructions, and letting users figure out the rest will result in lots of frustration, a lack of enjoyment, and many people giving up on their project.

Make it clear from the start that assistance is available. Whichever types of assistance you decide to offer, do your best to publicize and market them. When patrons inquire about digitization, let them know how willing staff is to help, and point them in the right direction for scheduling assistance.

Do your best to connect them with others in the community who are working on similar projects, or encourage them to recruit a friend to work alongside with, so they can support each other and learn together.

Make It Straightforward

Not only should the process be meaningful, but it also needs to be straightforward. Making it understandable, easy to digest and follow is crucial to ensuring a positive experience for everyone involved.

Many people you assist will have certain anxieties about technology. They will be unfamiliar with the equipment or other basics, or will have had bad experiences in the past, such as lost data. By breaking down the process into steps, clarifying certain jargon, and having a helpful attitude, you can ensure that the process is not only meaningful, but straightforward.

PREPARATION

Before you start working on your digitization project, it is always important to know what your ultimate goal is. It is not usually a wise idea to sit down at the scanner with a handful of slides, dial in some settings and digitize the files.

Having a clear goal helps the process go smoothly and results in a more organized, coherent collection of memories and historical documents. It also determines which settings you will choose when digitizing your materials.

If you are not sure how much storage you will need, having a rough idea of the quantity of items you'll be digitizing will help in determining these needs. This will also allow you to start thinking about data redundancy, file naming conventions, and other methods for making sure your data is safe, and easy to find and access.

Parameters like the resolution, file size, file format, and quality of your digitized file all depends on exactly what you intend to do with them. For example, if you just need a handful of photos scanned to display on a blog or webpage to send to friends or family, the settings you choose for those files will be different than for a larger collection of photos that you are digitizing and preserving for generations to come.

If time is an issue, you might also go with similar settings in order to get your digitized files in place in the proper amount of time. However, having ample time to settle into the process and learn the ins and outs of the equipment allows you to play around with the settings to figure out what works best for your media.

Chapter 2

Getting Started

Laying the groundwork for your digitization program is an important step in getting everything up and running. Making sure that you have the support, funding, and guidance necessary will ensure success for everyone involved. Before you consider purchasing software or equipment, assessing the foundations of your program will get you off on the right foot.

INSTITUTIONAL BUY-IN

Before you worry about the technical details, the space, and other items, you will want to get your organization and the community on board. This makes all the other steps that much easier. By having the right people invested, you will have the support, funding, guidance, and help needed to start a successful digitization program.

Support for Local History

Chances are your library already has some sort of local history collection or genealogical services. Think of the digitization program as an extension of those. You can sell it as building upon something you already have in place, and as a way to engage the community more in a service you already offer. Make sure to sell the service as central to what your library does, and that it builds community and engages residents with their past.

If you are fortunate, your organization's administration will be supportive and understand the benefits of such a program. By starting small, you can ease into a wider array of digitization offerings, not to mention getting the initial funding to show what a success such a service can be.

Funding

Funding is usually the first thing that comes to mind when considering a new library service. Fortunately, starting a DIY digitization program can be very affordable, even for libraries with tighter, smaller budgets. Equipment-wise, it does not take much to get off the ground. If you have the willingness to learn and a small budget, a digitization program is still within reach for your library.

For example, the Epson Perfection V600, a very popular flatbed scanner, used in many digital media labs, runs about $200. If you have a spare computer, this is all the equipment you would need to get a bare-bones operation started. Even if you need to purchase a computer for your digitization program, you can get started for under $1,000.

If funding is short, you have a few other options. One would be to try partnering with another organization in your community, such as a historical museum, to combine resources, and work together to bring digitization to your residents.

The digital media lab at the Arlington Heights Memorial Library (AHML), where I have run our digitization program, secured funding from our Friends of the Library, through its book sales and donations. If your library has a Friends, or book sales, you too can try to seek funding that way.

Donations are also another alternative. When we tried offering a way to digitize 8mm and Super 8mm films, in addition to old projectors we purchased from eBay, we were offered projectors from a few residents who heard what we were trying to do. With these donations, we were able to get the service off the ground. While we ultimately decided to postpone film digitization until better equipment could be secured (old projectors are difficult to get working properly and safely with residents' film), those donations helped set the groundwork for a better version of the service, and helped several patrons digitize some access copies of their films in the meantime.

Support from IT

Having your information technology (IT) staff on board will be a great help to your program. Depending on your setup, this may not require much assistance from IT, but having them involved from the start will make things easier for both sides.

Let us say you are going with a very straightforward scanning setup. All this requires is a space, a computer, and a scanner. IT will need to make sure the computer has the specs for working with the scanner, install whichever software the scanner came with, the drivers, and any editing software you would like, and you should be good to go. Scanners tend to be low-maintenance devices, so you will likely seldom need IT support for fixing issues.

If you have got a more in-depth digital media lab, or are going with a large setup and more equipment, IT will likely be involved more, both in the planning and in equipment purchasing process, as well as for supporting ongoing issues with any equipment that acts up.

Since most of the equipment that digitization focuses on will be administered by your library's IT staff, you will want to involve them from the very beginning. The last thing either party wants is any surprises. It is important for both sides to be understanding of the various goals for the digitization program. While you are concerned about functional, easy-to-use equipment and a great patron experience, your IT staff is probably concerned with security, reliability, and how the equipment you hope to purchase will fit in with the existing network and technological framework.

One of the first things that will determine what challenges IT will face is the platform you choose to go with. In other words, Mac or Windows. A Windows setup within an already-existing Windows-centric framework will be easier to manage, and the same goes for a Mac within a Mac-centric system. Introducing a different platform will require IT to develop a new administration strategy for your new setup, as well as prepare for the inherent risks of that platform.

For smaller digitization setups, this may be an easy choice. If you are going with one or two computers, and have no real need for either the advantages of a Mac or Windows setup, you can easily choose whatever fits into your system's current design. You may, however, be limited to a Windows setup if your scanner or other digitization equipment's software is developed only for the Windows platform. It is only when you venture beyond digitization, to more of a general digital media lab setup, that you may benefit from some Mac specific software, such as Garageband (audio production) and iMovie (video production) that are popular in many library media labs.

Make sure to involve IT from the beginning to avoid getting too involved or attached to any particular setup, only to find out that it will not be a good fit. It will help to see the process from IT's point of view. Every new computer or piece of equipment is a possible risk to the network and its security. This is IT's main concern, and they will make decisions with that in mind. In the long run, the security of the library's network and staff data is IT's responsibility, so its decision-making process will revolve around this mentality.

By working with them from the get-go and understanding their priorities, both parties will be able to achieve the results they are looking for. Not to mention, they will help you assess any compatibility or capability concerns regarding your new equipment.

Tech Education

Setting up a digitization service also provides you with the opportunity to tackle another service many libraries are offering or hope to offer: tech education. Not only does staffing your digitization service inherently bring in tech education opportunities, but it gives you the chance to evolve that into something more formal, such as one-on-one appointments and classes.

With many libraries shifting their attention from mainly providing services focused on books and information, many have shifted resources to education. Tech education has now become a priority in some organizations.

In fact, according to iPAC and ALA's 2013 Digital Inclusion survey, nearly 100 libraries in the United States are offering "workforce development training programs, online job resources, and technology skills training" (Wright, 2014). Digitization provides a great opportunity for giving the public, as well as library staff, the chance to learn new technologies.

You will find that tech education is a natural next-step after starting a digitization program. Residents will be hungry to learn more, and curious about how to not only begin digitizing their memories, but also taking it farther into more advanced projects that will be great learning experiences for them, as well as great opportunities for staff who are interested in teaching.

STAFFING

You now have the support needed for your digitization program, but how do you staff it? Do you hire someone or train a current employee? Do you let patrons fend for themselves at certain times and only staff the space during certain hours? There are a few options when it comes to staffing, but it is important to find what works for your library, your budget, and your patrons' needs. Proper staffing is a key ingredient in delivering great services and ensuring that residents will have a great experience with your new digitization service.

Training Current Staff

Many libraries stick with current staff for new services. While this is often because of budget constraints, it can definitely work.

This is an opportunity for someone to head up a new service or program, as well as learn about new technologies, and hone his or her customer service skills. With many new librarians or other library staff looking to bring their tech skills to the table, heading up a new digitization service should prove to be a great opportunity for these employees. This role might appeal to anyone looking for more teaching experience, to share his or her love of history and genealogy, or anyone who enjoys sharing his or her tech skills with others.

If multiple people are needed to staff the service, this could also be a growth opportunity for someone looking to lead a team of others—for example, a tech-focused librarian supervising a team of volunteers to deliver great service through the digitization program.

Hiring New Staff

Hiring new staff for digital media labs, makerspaces, or other tech-related services is often new territory for a library. Many libraries have opted to search for librarians with appropriate tech experience, while others have decided to hire outside of the field for someone with a tech-focused career. You will often find people with backgrounds in IT, graphic design, video production, audio production, and other tech or creative careers staffing these new spaces.

My own experience in libraries aligns with the latter. In 2012, the AHML piloted a new digital media lab, called the Studio. With an upcoming renovation, and the success of the pilot lab, they decided to hire a full-time staff member to help design the new space, plan out new services, manage the equipment and lab, and train staff and the public on new technologies. Fortunately for me, I was offered the job.

My background is mostly in digital media. I have a Bachelor of Arts in Visual Communication Design, plenty of experience in studio and live-sound production, have had my hands in several video projects, an all around competency with technology an general, and ample customer service experience. The position has been a great melding of all my skills.

The rest of the department I am part of, Digital Services Group, is mostly non-librarian. Everyone is expected to be able to support all services we offer (OverDrive, 3M Cloud Library, Zinio, hoopla, etc.), as well as basic computer, mobile and tablet skills, and other general technical knowledge. For AHML, hiring outside of the industry has been a great help. Our Digital Services department consistently receives great feedback from the public, and has been able to offer the community not only a DIY digitization service, but also an entire digital media lab, computer lab, and training center to offer them a wide range of tech skills and opportunities.

That is not the answer for every library, though. Budgetary reasons are often at the top of the list of hiring considerations, and if hiring outside of the industry does not make sense, more and more library students today have great tech knowledge. Many have experience in coding and development, others media production, and some content management and user experience. These are all great skills and knowledge to have when setting up a DIY digitization program.

Volunteers

One of the greatest assets any library has are the volunteers who give their time in service of the public. AHML has an indispensable group of volunteers who are great in assisting with programs, book sales, classes, and genealogy.

It is that last one where they can really tie in well with a digitization program. More than likely, some of the volunteers who assist your library have an interest in genealogy, local history, or digitization.

Volunteers in a library digitization lab should have two skills. First, they should have a basic or intermediate level of digitization knowledge. Second, they need to be able to instill this expertise in the public. They also need good customer service skills and knowledge of library policies.

Anyone of any age could contribute. Libraries could recruit staff from the local senior center or the high school. Students could possibly earn community service time or independent study credit.

HOW FAR DOES SUPPORT GO?

Providing great customer service is the foundation of any great library, but knowing where to draw the line with tech support is always a tough call. On one hand, we would love to see the customer through until his or her tech needs have been addressed. On the other hand, we cannot offer the level of service that professional tech support organizations do; otherwise, our appointments may never end, and staff training may become exhausting.

For example, having solutions to issues that often come up, (maybe a specific error that a scanner regularly gives, or issues in saving files to an external hard drive,) are helpful to have for the users who consistently encounter them (assuming these are bugs in the software and there is no easy fix) Do the research you can to provide additional support, but be realistic.

You will often find that beyond basic troubleshooting and support, the knowledge required for additional issues can quickly escalate. Usually, there are just a handful of common issues that make up the bulk of problems customers will run into.

Wherever you decide to draw the line, make sure to clearly communicate these limitations to the customer. It makes the experience better for both parties if expectations are set from the start.

ASSESSING COMMUNITY NEEDS

What are the needs of the community when it comes to digitization? It is important to have an idea of what sorts of things the community would like to digitize, what sort of presence there is relating to genealogy and history, and how to engage the community with the new digitization services. If there are particular communities with a strong presence in your town, find out what their needs are.

Is there a particular medium that is most popular in your community? Talk to residents to find out what it is they would like to digitize most. Maybe many people have stacks of photos they would like to scan, while others might have boxes full of cassette tapes, old oral histories, or a large collection of VHS tapes. It is likely a mix of all of these, but you want to make sure to get relevant equipment and provide support for the formats your community wants to work with.

Be realistic as well. Most digitization programs can easily support popular, universal formats such as VHS tapes and photos. You will always get a small amount of people requesting other formats such as Betamax, Laserdisc, or reel-to-reel audio. If you can find a way to purchase equipment that will digitize them, that is great, but the more niche the format, the harder it will be to get equipment and support the ability to digitize them. It does not hurt to have some outside companies to refer these patrons to if they need to have more obscure formats digitized.

LEVEL OF TECHNICAL COMPETENCY

It is also important to assess your community's comfort level with technology. If you have been teaching computer classes for awhile, your residents may have a decent tech foundation. If not, make sure to factor that into your training. You want to make your program as accessible as possible to provide value and meaning to anyone who might be interested.

Do your best to provide guidance for those who are starting from scratch, as well as those who are computer literate, but just need a little jump-start to get his or her project going. Never make any assumptions about someone's level of tech knowledge. Be upfront about what he or she can expect, and ask him or her where they stand, comfort-wise, with what he or she is about to embark on.

SPACE

If you have got an old office available, or even a small corner or a spot in your current computer lab, you have the space to start your digitization program. The space will provide your patrons with an accessible, comfortable spot to work through their digitization projects. In general, the space will require cleanliness, ample space to work and organize materials, proper power for all the equipment, and Internet access.

Using Existing Space

One of the easiest and most cost-effective ways to get started is to use an existing space. Chances are that your DIY digitization program's launch will not conveniently coincide with a renovation or overhaul of your facilities.

Unless you are making more of a dedicated digital media lab or maker space, digitization works well in most rooms you would have access to. There are just a few things you will want to keep in mind.

Size of the Space

All you really need is space for a computer, scanner, or other small pieces of equipment that digitization calls for. This may fit in an office, or in a spare station in your computer lab. Obviously, if you are looking to have multiple stations, you will need a larger space. The main concern is to make it comfortable, with enough desk space for patrons to work with the equipment and the materials they bring in.

Private or Public

You will want to decide if your space will be out in the open, or more closed off with a sense of privacy. If your station is out in the open, you have the advantage of visibility. Patrons may ask about the station, the services, or your local history collection when they see someone working on digitizing their materials. This visibility can really draw people into using the service and trying it out themselves.

On the other hand, for those who are more private about their history, they may not feel comfortable working with their materials out in the open. If your space is public, you can seek to balance that with a sense of privacy, by using dividers or low walls to make users feel like they have their own space.

Cleanliness

When working with old materials, you will want a space that is clean and easily managed. It is a good idea to avoid windows and vents, and to keep the space clean so there is minimum environmental impact on your patrons' materials.

Creating a New Space

If you are fortunate enough to have the opportunity to build a new space from scratch, you will have much more control over the experience.

There are a few things to keep in mind when designing a space from scratch. Again, will the space be public or private? Privacy offers the patron an opportunity to get comfortable, more in the zone, and connect with his or her materials in a more intimate way. It also allows you to control factors like cleanliness and dust more.

A public space will draw attention to your services. It will draw other patrons in to question and engage with the digitization process. In this way, you can also tie it in with any displays of local history you may already have. You can even consider making the equipment and process available as part of a local history exhibit to really make it interactive.

Maybe multiple rooms can be of benefit. Consider a room or corner that is more public facing, with elements that will engage people as they pass by, with access to private rooms.

Keep the ambience in mind as well. Private rooms can quickly become sterile, uninspiring, and closed off. Artwork, colors, or other decorations and environmental elements can help stave off a sense of isolation when in private. On the other hand, if your space is in public, offering headphones, or a simple wall divider may give patrons the sense of privacy or comfort they need when working.

HARDWARE AND SOFTWARE

The gear we use is only so important, especially for a DIY program. We are not usually looking at the top of the line equipment, just some options to aid in digitizing our materials.

For your residents, average equipment is more than enough. While we aim to make high-quality digitized copies of our memories and history, the main idea is to have a good enough copy to preserve the ideas behind our history. We are mainly talking computers, scanners, analog to digital converters and some other items.

You may also want to consider if staff and patrons will be sharing the same equipment, or if funding allows for each to have dedicated scanners. If both will be sharing, make sure to keep that in mind when choosing a space, managing time in the lab, and privacy and security concerns regarding your materials.

Chapter 3

What to Digitize

Almost anything can be digitized these days, in one form or another. Based on the needs of the community, you will be able to make a decision about what forms of media you will want to be able to digitize. Maybe your community has a very active genealogy group, so photos and documents would be a natural focus. If the spread is pretty even, you can do your best to offer services for photos, video, and audio.

Or, if you are forward-thinking and have the financial and technological support, look into three dimensional (3D) scanning as a way to digitize 3D objects and put a new spin on what people have in mind for digitization. Whatever it is your community is looking for, seek out ways to support them.

WHAT TO DIGITIZE: AN INTERVIEW WITH KATHY MARQUIS AND LESLIE WAGGENER

We will start this chapter out with something a little different. Kathy Marquis, the public service librarian at the Albany County Public Library in Wyoming, and Leslie Waggoner, the Simpson Institute Archivist at the American Heritage Center at the University of Wyoming in Laramie, were kind enough to answer some questions about what to collect for your library's Local History Reference Collection (LHRC), which can tie into your DIY digitization program.

Local History Reference Collections, by Kathy Marquis and Leslie Waggener

1. Can you introduce yourselves?

I'm Kathy Marquis. I've worked for most of my career as a reference archivist, in university archives and special collections in Massachusetts and Michigan, and in a large historical society (that was also the state archives) in Minnesota. For the past 13 years, I worked as the public services librarian at the public library in Laramie, Wyoming, directing reference, programming and selection for adults. I also ran the Wyoming Room, our local history reference collection, for most of my time there. It was a lot of fun for me to discover what reference in libraries and archives had in common—quite a lot, as I always suspected!

In 2015, Leslie and I were lucky enough to have the American Library Association publish our book, *Local History Reference Collections for Public Libraries*. Many of the answers to your questions will come from the research and writing we did for that book.

And, I'm Leslie Waggener. I'm an archivist at the University of Wyoming's American Heritage Center (AHC). Over the 15 years I've been at the AHC, I've worked with photographs, as well as many other types of historical materials in areas of reference, processing, and acquisition. I also worked as the Alan K. Simpson Institute Archivist, planning symposia and conducting oral histories on western U.S. economics and political topics.

2. How long have you been involved with collecting historical materials?

I began my archival career in 1975, as page (retriever) for the Bentley Historical Library at the University of Michigan. Specializing in reference for so long, I didn't acquire new materials for the archives where I worked. Then, in my last job at the public library (2002–2015), I was asked to manage the Wyoming Room. I was also the adult materials selector, so I kept my eyes out for publications, DVDs, and ephemeral material that could be added to the Wyoming Room and/or the circulating collection.

I came to the archival field in what might be called a jagged line instead of a straight shot. I was working as an archaeologist for the U.S. Forest Service in 1997 when a government shutdown laid off the archaeology crew. At a loss as to where to go next, I decided to volunteer at the small local library in my community. Knowing my interest in history, the library director asked me to organize their local history collection. After doing so, I was hooked! Archives became my profession of choice. I graduated with a MLIS from the University of Texas at Austin in 2000, and took a job at the University of Wyoming's American Heritage Center. I have been at the AHC for 15 years and have been involved in many phases of archival work, including reference, processing, acquisitions, oral history, and a dabble in digitization.

3. What's the difference between a LHRC and an archive? And, what are the most common materials worth collecting in an LHRC?

As defined by the Society of American Archivists, archives are "the materials created or received by a person, family, or organization, public or private, in the conduct of their affairs and preserved because of the enduring value contained in the information or as evidence of their functions and responsibilities of their creator, especially those materials maintained using the principles of provenance, original order, and collective control."[1]

Individuals can accumulate correspondence, diaries, photographs, and memoirs, as well as career-based materials such as speeches, drafts of books, research files, and business records. Organizations, companies, and corporations can accumulate some of the same materials, but their records can also include items pertaining to marketing, communications, and legal and financial decisions. Unlike what you'll find in a local history reference collection, most archival materials will be unpublished.

What we have come to call the Local History Reference Collection, or LHRC, is the type of resource area that just about any library can easily assemble and maintain. The focus is on published materials: books, periodicals (including newspapers), pamphlets, and print ephemera. Many of these, though certainly not all, might be donated to the library from the people or groups who have written them and would like to make sure that local citizens can find and make use of them. In our book, we emphasize the value of creating a collection development policy for your LHRC that allows you to politely decline materials, which don't really fit into your collection. Ephemeral items such as clippings, brochures, and flyers can be gathered into a traditional library vertical file. And all of these items can be reflected in the library's main online catalog (including the added entries created from the vertical file headings) so that the LHRC is not a mysterious or unexplored place in your library, but is discoverable like any other item in your collection.

For our book, we conducted a survey of public librarians about what we then called the "local history collection." But, in looking at the survey responses, we discovered that our concept and the term *local history collection* aren't necessarily synonymous in librarians' minds. Because of the acquisition of special or archival collections by many public libraries, local history collection has come to imply that unpublished materials are collected, or at least included. Thus, we chose to refer to our model as the local history *reference* collection to differentiate it.

Similarities—what archives and local history reference collections have in common:

- Attract similar researchers
- Support research/casual interest in genealogy and local history
- Materials can be found by searching the library's catalog
- Contain print and near-print materials
- Contain hard-to-replace, if not unique items
- Some materials in fragile condition
- Seen as "special" or separate
- Often have their own support groups, clubs, or Friends groups

The same people are likely to use both archival and local history reference collections. Librarians call them "patrons." Archivists call them "researchers." They can be, for example, grade school students working on a History Day project, students at any other level working on papers, lawyers researching a tricky land case, someone doing a history of his or her church, a railroad buff, or a scholar doing a full-length book on local economic history.

Of course, they could also be a genealogist or even someone just browsing through local history.

In general, archival collections contain mostly unique materials. But, that doesn't mean that everything in an LHRC, by contrast, is replaceable. Take for example the 19th-century published county history, the city directories, or the beautifully illustrated, oversize county atlas. All were originally published in quantity. But, there are very few copies left now, and an LHRC collection probably has one of the few in decent shape. In this age of digitization, it is possible that some of these items have been scanned, and are even available in an online database to which your library system subscribes. However, it is unlikely that this will be true of all of the rare, research materials in your library's local history room. Keeping in mind the condition of the originals in one's care is something both public libraries and archives have in common. Good preservation techniques, and careful education of patrons, constitute the stewardship responsibilities that both venues have in common.

In short, archives and local history reference collections share many of the same users, research interests, print and near-print source materials, discovery mechanisms, and supporters. In fact, some archival institutions have small print collections of secondary materials related to their collecting areas (e.g., railroads or women's history), which could look quite similar to a typical public library local history reference collection.

Differences:

- Most of an archival collection is unique material while an LHRC's collection is largely published
- Archival collections are most commonly donated, rather than purchased
- Size and description: archival collections can be huge, and are described at the collection, not item level in the catalog
- Processing archival material can necessitate separate space to organize the materials
- They require special housing, climate, and humidity controls
- Physical access to the collections: Is browsing possible (LHRC) or are there locked stacks (archives)?
- Providing access and security: Archivists place limits on the number of items available at one time, require retrieval and copying by staff, ask patrons to register and lock up their possessions, and there is an intermediary step of checking the archival finding aid listing to find what to request.

While some items in LHRCs may be donated by patrons, most of the published items will need to be purchased. This is another significant difference from archival collections, which solicit or accept donations for almost all of their collection materials. Rather than selecting materials from vendors, catalogs, or reviews, archivists acquire collections through requests to individuals or groups. Of course, some archival collections, generally from well-known individuals, may need to be purchased. But this is the exception, not the rule.

Getting a small archive started, and maintaining it, requires resources not usually needed for a local history reference collection. Here are some examples:

- Archival collections need room to be processed into separate boxes.
- Finding aids (descriptions and contents lists) need to be prepared so researchers can discover what the collections contain.
- Secured storage space is required to house the boxes, preferably in a climate-controlled room. And a higher level of security is needed when archival materials are being used by researchers; a separate research space is essential so a watchful eye can be kept on these unique materials.
- A dedicated room for research with local history reference materials is worthwhile so that local history materials aren't carted all over the library. But with archival material, it's essential. Archival materials are unique; replacing an item is usually impossible.

Access is a considerably more complicated process when it comes to archival material. A patron who simply walks into the local history reference collection and finds materials she needs will need to do the following at a minimum in an archive: lock up belongings, present ID and register, and search a catalog that will point to the collections of interest. A researcher discovers what a collection contains through reviewing its finding aid,[2] which provides a short biographical piece, a scope and content note, and a listing of series, usually organized box by box, indicating what is in the papers.

The finding aids must be searched for specific boxes of interest and call slips filled out. The archives staff will then retrieve the requested boxes from closed stacks. They may ask the student to wear gloves to handle any photographs in the collection. Making sense of the information found can often depend on previous secondary source research and any photocopies will most likely need to be made by staff. This can be a very alienating—though ultimately rewarding—process. It is one of the most significant differences, at least from the patrons' point of view, between library local history sections and archives.

Unlike for those who manage an LHRC, *provenance* is a big deal to archivists. In order to maintain context, archivists keep materials from one creator together and don't rearrange materials (e.g., by subject.). Another *big* difference is size. Archival collections often consist of hundreds of boxes—measured in cubic feet. Archival storage areas can be massive—and they are closed to users. No browsing through the aisles of boxes. This places more emphasis in archives on the staff as intermediaries, while libraries strive to make patrons as self-sufficient as possible.

5. Which items tend to be in the best condition?

The items in the best condition are most likely to be the more recently published monographs you select. Your LHRC should include all the new research that your community is (hopefully!) producing, such as histories of your town, region, ethnic groups, businesses, churches, and so forth. Of course, you may well have noticed that current hardbound books are not bound as well as they once were. So, a 50-year-old book, with carefully sewn signatures may actually last much longer than a book you bought last year.

6. What's most difficult to preserve?

The two categories in most danger are items on newsprint (newspapers and ephemera) and audio-visual materials. Acid is the great degrader of paper. Paper produced after the Civil War is generally higher in acid content and it crumbles easily, especially after exposure to light and/or low humidity. AV items such as locally produced DVDs, videotapes collected in previous decades, and other items require temperature and humidity stability, as well as cleaning and sometimes reformatting.

Because of the instability of these acidic and magnetic media, it's wise to consider reformatting the items you think warrant the time and expense. Reformatting newsprint single items in your vertical file can be as simple as photocopying the items onto higher-quality paper. Most (but, of course not all) public and academic libraries these days have the most basic of temperature and humidity controls: heat in the winter and air conditioning in the summer. This will represent much greater stability for the paper than it might have had in someone's attic or basement, before it was collected by the library.

In our survey, and at library conferences, we have encountered quite a bit of interest on the part of public librarians in starting special projects to digitize copies of their local newspapers. Before you begin such a project—or seek funding to do it—please consult your state archives and/ or state library. Many states have already undertaken massive newspaper microfilming and/ or digitization projects of which you may be unaware. All you have to do is purchase the microfilm reels, or in many cases, link the digitized files to your library's catalog or website. An excellent place to start is this list of historical newspapers online, compiled by the librarians at the University of Pennsylvania: http://viewshare.org/views/refhelp/. Save all that energy for items that have not already been preserved!

7. What are some of the most interesting items you've come across?

The most unusual items listed by our survey respondents were definitely the variety of artifacts such as arrowheads, fishing ties, and even street signs, telephones, and swords. We were really torn about collecting items like these. On the one hand, a tiny number of unusual objects make for great displays and can draw attention to your collection. On the other hand, like archival materials, artifacts require careful handling and storage, possibly more than your library is willing to support.

In our opinion, collecting these items also leads to what has been called "mission creep." We strongly recommend taking the time to craft a collecting policy for your collection, considering in advance what you truly want to have, and care for—and then sticking to it, even when patrons offer items outside your policy. You are actually doing them a favor in finding an appropriate archival or museum repository for their treasured heirloom than if you take it and, not knowing quite what to do with it, make it inaccessible or subject to mishandling or loss. Another way to offer sound professional advice is to help them keep the items safe and well cared for in their own family homes. Sometimes items have considerably more significance to their family than for historical study, particularly if they are in rough shape or no one knows their provenance (where they came from.) Helping your patrons locate information and expertise (like conservators or vendors of archival storage containers) so they can continue to cherish these items is a most valuable service you can provide.

8. Any library programs or displays for an LHRC that stick out?

There are so many inventive ways to showcase your LHRC, and we found that libraries could be very creative in using their materials—and their staff expertise—for outreach and publicity. However, we'd like to focus here on some of the ways that libraries are using social media to get their LHRCs out there.

Some are little known applications, and others are "mashups": combining several applications or content from one source viewed in contrast or concert with another. Kate Theimer in her *Web2.0 Tools and Strategies for Archives and Local History Collections* notes, "The overwhelmingly predominant use of mashup technology among archives is to combine information about objects in the collections with geographic data."[3] We also found this to be true of local history collections.

The Albany (New York) Public Library's LHRC has created Android/Apple apps for local history, allowing patrons to use their phones as a walking tour guide using maps and old photographs of the city.[4]

The Onondaga County (New York) Public Library is using its Instagram account to showcase its visual content. We like to point out that all attractive content is not photographic; many libraries are finding historic print material that is just as eye-catching.[5]

There were fewer timelines than we would have predicted. Matt Enis's recent *Library Journal* article contained a review of a handful of timeline software options. See "Time After Time, Product Spotlight" for an overview of several current timeline applications.[6] The Oak Lawn (Illinois) Public Library used an app called "Capzles" for its timeline.[7]

Like many apps, it takes your content and plugs it into a program providing easy navigation for your patrons.

The city of Orange, California, has a fun section called "History's Mysteries" with unidentified photos[8] and the Austin Public Library recast its local history FAQ as a quiz.[9] While not technically a social media applications, they are certainly encouraging patron interaction and engagement with their resources and staff.

Several libraries created map and photograph mash-ups to show local historic site locations. The library in Franklin Park, Illinois, has used Google maps, while the Kalamazoo Public Library has created an interactive map using a lesser-known app called "Tagwhat."[10]

The Oak Lawn (Illinois) Public Library has used both Google maps and U.S. Geological Survey maps to show different facets of its community history. And they have used photos in their Flickr account to create a "Then and Now" exhibit of local views, all in Historypin.[11]

The important thing to remember is that these are all ways to repurpose your digitized content. They are not storage solutions. Social media companies come and go with some frequency. Take advantage of all the outreach opportunities they offer, but make sure that your files are safely stored elsewhere so that you can continue to use them as you choose.

9. Which libraries have some of your favorite LHRCs?

To be honest, we didn't find a lot of local history reference collections in our research. Most were traditional local history collections with manuscript and archival materials. However, we would like to mention the Indiana Room at the Anderson (Indiana) Library (http://www.and.lib.in.us/research-genealogy). They have a well-stocked and well-staffed collection that is built around the traditional library publications and ephemera that we recommend in our book. They link to lots of great local history databases, and they do programs for genealogists as well.

10. What other community organizations may be able to help you build an LHRC?

The first groups which come to mind are the local genealogical society and historical society, and your own Friends of the Library group. The first two are comprised of people who naturally care about local history and the history of local families. Some ways you might work with them include planning joint events, asking them to host their own meetings or events in your library, asking for time in their meeting agendas to talk about your LHRC, and using each other's mailing lists and PR venues to cross publicize. Local authors groups also can be a big support—and a source for collection items.

Once you have a collecting policy and are settled on what types of materials you are looking to collect (and not collect) local history/genealogy groups are great avenues for making appeals for donations of materials. They may have county histories or maps or city directories that they can't store or care for as well as you can. Their members may be able to alert you to patrons doing local history research—who might want to donate a copy of their finished product to you. In some cases, such societies either donate their entire research collections to the public library's local history reference collection, or they collaborate in other ways. The genealogical society members might be willing to volunteer to help your patrons on a regular basis. This helps their membership base, as well as giving your patrons more expert assistance.

Finally, cooperative or collaborative relationships with these groups can also result in financial donations to the library, earmarked for your collection. Any fund-raising you are allowed to do should include these groups both in planning and outreach.

The same goes for your Friends group. If they take used book donations and run a sale, they can be your scouts for likely additions to the LHRC. If they have a wider mandate, either in terms of programming and/or fund-raising, be sure that they know what the LHRC's needs are. You'll want to keep your director or development office in the loop, but with their say, so your Friends group can be your best friends.

The other major category of community groups would be any nearby archives, museums or libraries. Not only can you work together on events, and collaborative projects like digitization, but you can cooperate on selection and handling donations. If you have a good working relationship with these organizations, you can knowledgeably refer donors who have items that need the storage facilities of an archives or an interest in collecting objects of a museum. A second set of high school yearbooks might be a "no thanks" for the local historical society, but if they know you'd like a set for your LHRC, they can refer the donor to you.

11. What interesting niches might a library focus on for an LHRC?

I guess we would say that the local history reference collection's niche is its own local history. This may seem obvious, but most collections have the tendency to broaden in focus over time. We recommend narrowing the focus, instead. In the spirit of cooperation and non-competition with other local historical repositories (archives, museums, local historical society, etc.) it's useful to find out what their strengths are and make your collection complementary. For example, rather than collecting information on your entire region or state, keep it focused on your town or county. It's less likely that anyone else has this unique focus.

12. How might a library's DIY digitization program tie in with collecting items for an LHRC?

Our main thought here is to be careful not to put out a generous call such as, "bring us your historical materials and we'll scan them for you!" We have heard from a county historical society which tried this approach at a county fair booth. They were inundated with requests which they had no way to appraise or evaluate for fitness for their collection. They ended up having to turn people away which was the exact opposite of what they had intended. There was also no good way to collect descriptive metadata on the items.

Nonetheless the promise of digitization can encourage donations. The key is to have a clear idea; first, which items you might want to acquire. This method can also allow you to "accept" for the collection fragile items by incorporating the access or surrogate digital copy without having to care for the item which might be in need of much conservation work—and also might have ongoing value to the family which brought it to you.

13. Can you tell us about what kinds of information you try to get for each item in your collections? And do you catalog them, or tag them with metadata?

We absolutely advocate the inclusion of records in the central library catalog for all materials, including those in a local history or local history reference collection. For the patron, the simplest path to the discovery of your collection is through the mechanism he or she is already familiar with: your catalog. Too many local history collections have layers of guides, lists, and indices to pieces of their holdings. At the very least, catalog the lists!

Probably the most surprising discovery we made via our survey of public librarians was in this area. Most discrete monographs were cataloged, but as soon as the format seemed different or "special," librarians assumed that the familiar MARC cataloging conventions would not work for these materials. Many, in fact, had purchased separate, proprietary databases such as Past Perfect (the most commonly named, though it was created for museum collections.) In the process, they established yet another place for their patrons to seek local history information, which is counterintuitive at best.

As it happens, archivists and manuscript curators use the MARC cataloging conventions as librarians to create records, at the group or collection level, for their holdings. There are some new fields to learn, but instead of starting from scratch with a whole new system, it makes more sense to learn some new fields and integrate your information into the catalog you already have.

The answer to the first question about information to seek depends on the format of the item or group. If it is a monograph, look for all the same identifiers as usual. You might pay special attention to locally significant place or personal/corporate names (and you might have to establish them). If you are working with your technical services department, you could give them a break and help them identify some of the most significant local history names and topics, as you are more likely to be familiar with them.

In addition, archivists are beginning to catalog and create metadata for digitized objects at the collection or series level, as well (rather than for each item).[12] For anyone pursuing a digitization project, this is a development to watch. The last thing we want is to create whole new backlogs of undescribed digital collections.

PHOTOS, DOCUMENTS, AND WORKS ON PAPER

When you think of digitization, photos are usually first on the list. Photography has been around for two centuries, so we have plenty of history in our photographs. Not only that, but also in written letters, sketches, and other documents on paper.

Documents are far reaching, with a wide variety of formats that could prove valuable to someone's personal history or for the community. Some items include:

- Town, city, or village anniversary
- House, school, business, or church history/index
- Items from organizations such as Scouts, DAR, and VFW
- School transcripts
- Awards
- Diplomas
- Deeds
- Diaries and journals
- Yearbooks
- Church bulletins

VIDEO AND MOTION PICTURES

In this section, video refers to any sort of motion picture, whether it is proper video, like VHS tapes or MiniDV, but also reel-to-reel film, such as Super 8mm. This is not an exhaustive list, but covers many formats you may run into, including some basic information, such as how long the format has been around for, so you have an idea how old someone's materials may be. This can also help to avoid confusion over similar formats, such as 8mm and Hi8 tapes.

VHS Tape

This is the most common video format you will come across. Since they were the main consumer level format for more than two decades, starting in the late 1970s, many people will have their home videos on VHS Tapes.

They are inexpensive to support, since VCRs, and the newer VHS to DVD units are easy to come by, and very affordable.

Betamax Tape

Betamax tapes initially competed with VHS tapes, coming out in 1975, but eventually lost out, and are not as common to find.

Playback units are difficult to come by and more expensive, so this is not as viable an option for digitization.

8mm (Video8) Tape

This format debuted in the early 1980s as a smaller way to record video at the same quality as VHS. Many people have home movies in this format, as it was an early format for consumer level, home video recording equipment.

Hi8 Tape

Hi8 is an improved version of Video8, with better quality, but in the same form factor. Hi8 players can player the older Video8 format, but not the other way around.

Digital8 Tape

This format came out in 1999 and used the same tapes as Video8, but is otherwise completely different. It is a digital format, recorded in digital video (DV) as opposed to analog, like previous tape formats. Some Digital8 players can player the previous Video8 and Hi8 formats, but it is not universal.

MiniDV Tape

MiniDV uses smaller tapes than the previous 8mm formats, and is entirely digital. These tapes can be played only on MiniDV equipment. These were very popular in the 2000s, so you will find a fair amount of patrons who are looking to work with these. While they are technically already digital, people will want to convert them to DVDs or to video files for further editing.

DVD

The DVD format came out in 1997 and ended up replacing VHS tapes as the dominant consumer video format. DVD was the last format with standard definition (SD) video, although it was still much clearer than VHS tape.

Patrons with DVDs already have digital video, but may want to make copies or rip (a term used for converting disc based media to a digital file on a computer) it to a digital video file on the computer for further changes or editing.

Blu-Ray

Blu-Ray came out in 2006 as a competitor to HD-DVD, and ultimately won out as the successor to DVD. It is the same physical size and DVD, but wields greater, high definition (HD) quality video and audio.

Blu-Ray will come up seldom, since it has existed in the age of consumer level digital video. Because of this, most people will have the original source video for anything that may have been subsequently burned to Blu-Ray. Like DVD, they can also be ripped back to a computer.

16mm Film

In 1923, 16mm film came out as a format for amateur filmmakers and consumers. A projector is necessary to view the film. Stored properly, 16mm films can still be found in relatively good condition.

8mm Film

Debuting in 1932, 8mm film came onto the market as the next step in home video production. Since many in the boomer generation grew up with 8mm film, you may find a large demand for the ability to digitize this format.

Super 8mm Film

Super 8mm film came out in 1965, with the same size film, but with high-image quality and easier operation. Like 8mm and 16mm, Super 8mm film can be in good condition today if stored properly. If not, some films may be brittle and hard to work with.

Just like 8mm, Super 8mm was used by many people of boomer generation, so you may find a large demand for the ability to digitize this format.

AUDIO

Audio can be found on old cassette tapes or reel-to-reel setups. This is not an exhaustive list, but covers many formats you may run into, including some basic information, such as how long the format has been around for, so you have an idea how old someone's materials may be.

Cassette Tape

This is the most common format of tape that you will encounter with digitization projects. Offered at a consumer level since the 1970s, many people have valuable audio stored on cassette tapes. They also offered an early, affordable, and easy way to do recording at home, so some families have their own homemade recordings or oral histories in this format.

Vinyl

While not as many people will have home recordings on vinyl, since even to this day, the process of cutting vinyl is very expensive, there will still be records that people will want to digitize. The advantage of vinyl is that it is one of the most resilient forms of recording, rated to last up to 100 years or more if stored and cared for properly.

Reel-to-Reel Tape

When reel-to-reel tape hit the market, it came in several formats. Most likely, at the consumer level, you will see 1/4 inch tape, and possibly 1/2 inch tape. The larger formats, such as 1 and 2 inch tapes were used for multitrack recording in large, professional recording and broadcast studios.

Reel-to-reel poses challenges since working playback systems are hard to come by, but are necessary for digitization. Playback devices can be found on eBay, or possibly through patron donations.

DIRECT DIGITIZATION

When people first think of digitization, they usually think of old dusty photos, aging film, or music from another time. While there are all sorts of good material in older formats, digitization does not have to be limited to memories and events from the past. Digitization can happen right now, and the tools have never been better.

If you think about it, digitization, at its most basic level, is the conversion of media to a digital format. So, why not digitize the world, right at the source? Rather than take a photo, record music, or shoot video, and wait 50 years to transfer it to the current or most prominent media format of the time, why not consider it digitized at the moment you capture it on your smartphone or digital camera? Why not digitize the world directly?

In 2013, 90 percent of the world's data was created in just the previous two years (SINTEF, 2013). Through Flickr, Facebook, Instagram, Snapchat, and WhatsApp alone, we are uploading more than 1.8 billion photos a day (Edwards, 2014). With the mass amounts of data being generated on a daily basis, through e-mail, social media, and digital media, we are digitizing incredible amounts of information. This all tells the story of what is currently going on. Hundreds of years down the road, our descendants may seek out our tweets and blog entries in order to find the stories that made us, our cultures and our world.

The photos you take with friends while on vacation, the videos of your children's sports games, and the voicemails your loved ones leave you, these all count as digitized materials you may want to save.

So, consider your documentation worth preserving. Just because you did not scan it, does not mean it does not belong. Make sure to include your modern media in your plan for preservation. How will you back it up, along with your digitized materials from the past? How will you organize them with your other materials?

When working with patrons, make sure to bring this up. What aspects of their current digital lives might they want to preserve? And what is the best way to preserve it? How do you save things such as tweets, blog entries, websites, or other digital and web ephemera?

SAVING EPHEMERA FROM THE WEB AND SOCIAL MEDIA

History is made every day on the Internet. While much of it is noise, there is content worth saving, whether for larger historical reasons or for personal reasons. Not all services offer convenient way to save content, so sometimes a workaround is needed, such as taking a screenshot.

Tweets

In 2010, the Library of Congress announced it would be archiving all of Twitter's public tweets, giving future generations the ability to search and relive the cultural, social, and political trends of our time (Osterberg, 2013). It will not include private account information and deleted tweets, nor will it include linked content and websites.

Twitter actually offers a feature for downloading an archive of all your own tweets. To do so, go to your Twitter settings, and select *Request your archive.* Twitter will send you a download link at your e-mail address, and will supply a *Go now* link which will download your archive.

The result is an html file, which you can easily duplicate and backup. Twitter does not offer a service for saving other people's tweets, but websites like *twodocs.com* and *allmytweets.com* offer this facility.

Facebook Posts

Facebook offers the ability to download your information. Specifically, you can choose what information to include, such as profile info, photos, posts, and more. To do so, go to your Facebook settings, select *Download a copy of your Facebook data,* and click *Start My Archive.*

The result is an html file and all associated photos and links.

Blogs

Many blogs offer you the ability to download an archive of your posts and content. With the dynamic nature of the web and the quick pace at which things change, it is important to save a copy of your writings.

Popular blogs such as WordPress and Blogger offer this feature. In many cases, it is called exporting your blog. This option can often be found in the options or settings section. You will want to find what format it exports to, in case you want to import it to another publishing platform on the web.

Websites

In addition to blogs, our websites often contain very important content regarding our personal work, as well as valuable cultural and historical ephemera.

Depending how your site was built, you will want to look into creating a backup and archive. Services like WordPress offer the ability to create backups and download archives. Even if you are not using a web publishing platform, you can still log into your hosting service and download an entire copy of your website.

Screenshots and Clipping

In case you do not have formal access or control to the content you are trying to save, there are tools out there for saving screenshots and clippings of content from the web.

Popular services like Evernote offer this facility. Evernote lets you install an extension into your browser to save clippings—for example, photos, snippets of text, and other objects from the web that saves the content to your Evernote account.

Screenshots can be helpful as well. On the PC, you can hit the *Print Screen* button, paste the image into an image editor, and save the image. Alternatively, you can use the *Snipping Tool,* which conveniently lets you choose a portion of the screen to save, and quickly edit and save it.

On the Mac, clicking *Command + Shift + 4* will allow you to click and drag a box around the area you wish to save. *Command + Shift + 4 + Space* will let you snap specific windows.

Objects

While most of the focus of digitization up to this point has been on text, images, audio, and video, we can begin to look toward what is next. In recent years, libraries have moved beyond those traditional formats and into the 3D realm. You will now find makerspaces and digital media labs across the country, many of them with 3D printers. Some offer 3D scanning as well.

There are now affordable options for scanning our 3D objects and storing their likeness in a file, able to be used for printing a copy. While a 3D scan does not provide a copy in the same way that scanning an image, or digitizing a video does, it gives you a way to preserve the shape, size, and likeness of a given object. This still provides value and meaning, and offers a way to engage with the object even more, through manipulation and correction of the 3D model itself.

NOTES

1. Richard Pearce-Moses, *A Glossary of Archival and Records Terminology* (Chicago: Society of American Archivists, 2005). http://www2.archivists.org/glossary

2. An example of a finding aid is here: http://quod.lib.umich.edu/cgi/f/findaid/findaid-idx?c=bhlead&idno=umich-bhl-851100. It is for the records of the Detroit Urban League, a social service organization serving the Detroit African American community.

3. Kate Theimer, *Web 2.0 Tools and Strategies for Archives and Local History Collections* (New York: Neal-Schuman Publishers, 2010): 180.

4. https://play.google.com/store/apps/details?id=com.troyweb.albanyhistory&feature=search_result#?t=W251bGwsMSwxLDEsImNvbS50cm95d2ViLmFsYmFueWhpc3RvcnkiXQ

5. https://instagram.com/lhg_ocpl/

6. Matt Enis, "Time After Time | Product Spotlight," *Library Journal,* vol. 139, no. 14 (2014): 34. http://lj.libraryjournal.com/2014/09/digital-content/time-after-time-product-spotlight/#

7. http://www.capzles.com/#/33c0b0c7-a50d-4b27-aa46-e1a725da5094/

8. http://www.cityoforange.org/localhistory/default.htm

9. http://library.austintexas.gov/ahc/austin-quiz

10. http://www.kpl.gov/local-history/tagwhat/

11. https://www.historypin.org/channels/view/36484/

12. Ricky Erway and Jennifer Schaffner, *Shifting Gears: Gearing Up to Get Into the Flow* (OCLC: 2007). http://www.oclc.org/content/dam/research/publications/library/2007/2007-02.pdf

Chapter 4

The Equipment

Now things are getting concrete. We have the institutional buy-in, the financial backing, and the need has been identified in the community. It is time to begin looking at purchasing the equipment.

Understandably, the actual equipment can be intimidating to those who find themselves unfamiliar with certain technology, but with patience and an open mind, your average digitization equipment can be easy to use.

HARDWARE

For digitizing photos, slides, film and documents, we are mainly looking at scanners. Chances are, you have used one before, or have one at home, even as part of an all-in-one printer. Scanners have been at the consumer level for about two decades, so these will be the most familiar.

For video, we are also looking at devices we are already familiar with, such as VHS players, DVD players or other playback devices for various formats of the past. The newer equipment is usually a small box called an A/D converter, or analog to digital converter. This is what converts a video signal from it is original analog domain to the digital world.

Finally, for audio, we are also looking at devices you have most likely used before, such as turntables or cassette decks. This might also entail using an A/D converter, often referred to as an interface in this case, or a new breed of cassette deck or turntable that has digitization capabilities built in. These connect via USB to your computer just like a flash drive or hard drive.

We will also touch on even older formats, such as reel-to-reel film, like 8mm or Super 8mm, as well as reel-to-reel audio. These formats require either aging equipment that still functions, or more expensive, but new equipment, specially designed to digitize these old formats. There are a few DIY workarounds as well that will be covered.

Scanners

Scanners have been around for quite some time. They are the workhorses of digitization. Usually, when we think of preserving our materials, photos are the first thing that comes to mind. With the advent of photography back in early 1800s, we are coming up on nearly two centuries of photography, so it offers us a rich history of ourselves and our cultures. Because of this, photos tend to be the most ubiquitous of materials that patrons may bring in.

The process for scanning is relatively straightforward as well. Photos are usually scanned one at a time, with a specific range of settings, and the result is a digital file, usually a JPEG or TIFF.

Once you know your budget, you can better figure out what type of scanner you can afford, and what trade-offs to make. Most scanners require an accompanying computer with appropriate software to run the scanner.

For example, if you would like a scanner that needs to be only able to scan mostly aging documents and a handful of photos, you can narrow the search and focus on scanners with features that are tailored to those materials. However, if some of these documents are larger sizes, you know you will have to focus on a scanner that has a larger flatbed. Many popular scanners do not accommodate materials larger than 11 × 14 inches.

Flatbed

For most purposes, and for DIY digitization programs, you will be dealing with flatbed scanners. These are large, flat machines, usually only a few inches tall, around two-feet deep and a foot wide, with a large pane of glass under the lid, atop which you place your photos, documents, slides, or film.

Some flatbed scanners are meant for documents, others have high-quality imaging components for photographs, and others include the capability to scan slides and film negatives.

For most purposes, these scanners work fine. They range in price from under $100 to thousands for high-end image scanners. The scanners that reside in the $100–$500 price range are just fine for the type of scanning the members of your community will be doing. Many of these include the ability to scan photos, documents, slides, and film negatives.

If you have a scanner already, chances are this is the type you have, and if not, there is a good chance this is the type you will end up with. They range from affordable and straightforward to expensive and more advanced.

They can be large devices, so you will want to make sure you have enough desk space for your scanner. Depending on what you will be helping people digitize, size can play a role. Many scanners are large enough for letter and legal documents, but if you will be scanning larger and more irregular sized documents, you may want to look into a larger sized flatbed.

Some flatbeds allow you to scan multiple forms of media, such as documents and photos, as well as film negatives and slides. The scanners that allow you to scan film and slides, or transparencies, have a backlight built into the lid. A backlight is necessary for scanning transparent media. They come with trays that help you position and place your transparencies in the correct spot on the flatbed's glass.

Other flatbeds include software with the capability for optical character recognition, or OCR. OCR is able to scan an image of text and convert it into selectable text that can be copied and pasted into a word processor for editing. This is great if you have old documents you would like to edit or make changes to without retyping everything. The clearer the original type, the better results OCR will give you. Since it relies on detecting recognizable, consistent letterforms, handwriting will likely not work with it.

It is also good to keep in mind whether you are scanning an opaque document like a letter or photographic print, or a transparency like film and slides. Many flatbed scanners will state a maximum scan area, which refers to the size of the glass itself. However, other scanners that also include a function for scanning transparencies are only able to do so within a smaller area. A backlight is needed for this, which is built into the lid of the scanner. Sometimes it is as large as the maximum scan area, sometimes it is smaller.

When purchasing your scanner, you will want to make sure it will be able to connect to your computer and run the accompanying software as well. USB connections are near universal on these scanners, and most software will run on Windows and Mac platforms.

Specialty

While flatbed scanners are great for most projects, there are dedicated film, photo, and slide scanners that have different optics and electronics specifically geared toward these mediums. These can be a good choice if you know you will be working specifically with one medium, and if quality is of great importance.

For example, many digital media labs have dedicated film scanners, most likely for 35mm negatives. Unlike flatbeds, there is no open pane of glass for placing the negatives onto. Usually, there is a plastic tray that holds anywhere from a 5–10 photo strip of 35mm negative film. You will also be able to find similar scanners for opaque documents and slides.

Once the settings are dialed in on the software the scanner will digitize each frame of the strip. The equipment in these scanners, and settings in the software, are specialized for 35mm film.

Bulk

The scanners we have mentioned already are great for many jobs, but the biggest drawback is that they usually scan only one to a handful of images at once. You will encounter a sizable group of people who are interested in digitizing their entire collections.

While this is feasible over the long term, say scanning for a few hours once a week of the course of a year (which I have encountered many patrons doing), it is unrealistic and prohibitive for others.

Bulk scanners are much more expensive (usually $300–$5000), but they offer the convenience of scanning large quantities of slides, film, or photos, either more quickly, with less assistance, or with both.

Like specialty scanners, they are geared toward one medium in particular, so choose wisely. Most bulk scanners are for photos and documents, or slides, specifically. Bulk photo and document scanners often allow you to place a stack of images or papers into it, and it will automatically draw them through, scan them, and save them to a number of various formats. Some can do as few as 10 at a time, and some as many as 100 or more. Several bulk scanners can accommodate various sizes, usually common formats, such as letter, legal, business cards and envelopes, and so forth.

Bulk slide scanners often feature a proprietary slide tray that can hold 10–50 slides, or a more traditional carousel, from slide projectors to cycle through each image.

As with any piece of equipment, you will want to put your scanner through some trials before opening it up to the public. Bulk scanners, by nature, since they are automated, can run into issues mid-scan, such as jams, mis-feeds, and communication errors with the computer.

It is also worth mentioning that your library's copier(s) may already suit the functionality of the bulk scanner. While they do not offer the best quality, they can still be a great option for bulk scanning. Many new copiers have USB ports on them, and can scan single documents or large stacks of paper, even double sided, and can save them to a PDF. Make sure to look into the capabilities of your copier before purchasing any new equipment.

Book Scanners

For those who are looking to digitize bound materials, sometimes a flatbed scanner just will not cut it. The need to digitize hundreds of pages, pages larger than a scanner's image area, or the fragility of old volumes all point toward the need for a specific book scanner.

While the types of scanners many larger institutions have are prohibitively expensive, there are a few options for your new DIY digitization program. Because of their nature, they are larger in size than your average scanner, but still require a proper computer connection and accompanying software.

Scanner Recommendations

In my experience, building a digital media lab for my own library, working with other institutions to build their own labs, and in meeting with other lab managers, certain models standout. Others, I have not personally worked with, but seem to be good options for certain needs.

This list is by no means exhaustive, but serves as a way to begin your search for scanning equipment.

(Flatbed) Epson Perfection Photo V600—$229

For the flatbed, the Epson Perfection Photo V600 has been the go-to model for many libraries. The Studio, the digital media lab at the Arlington Heights Memorial Library (AHML) where I work, has two of these scanners, and they have been the bread and butter of our photographic and documentary digitization services. They are used multiple times a day, with a shallow learning curve, great reliability, and results that our customers are happy with.

- Maximum optical resolution of 6400 DPI
- Maximum scan area of 8.5 × 11.7
- Twelve 35mm negative film images simultaneously
- Four 35mm slide images simultaneously (Epson Perfection V600, 2015)

(Flatbed) Epson Perfection V700—$739.99

If you are looking for a step up in quality, and better capabilities for scanning transparencies, Epson also offers a good option with the Epson Perfection V700.

- Maximum optical resolution of 6400 DPI
- Dual lens scanning
- Maximum scan area of 8.5 × 11.7
- 8 × 10 transparency size
- Twenty-four 35mm negative film images simultaneously
- Twelve 35mm slide images simultaneously
- Six medium format frames simultaneously
- Two 4 × 5 frames simultaneously (Epson Perfection V700, 2015)

(Batch Scanner) PowerSlide 5000—$1,099.99

With this scanner, you get the convenience of being able to scan batches of 50 slides at a time. As with flatbed scanners, the time it takes to scan your slides depends on the settings that you plug into the software. The settings include resolution, exposure, color correction and so on.

For example, scanning slides at resolution of 1200 DPI with only auto exposure on ends up scanning at about two minutes per slide. You can scan about 60 slides in two hours. That is not the fastest way to scan slides but the fact that you can set it and forget it proves to be a big value when you are working on a large project.

- Batch scan 50 × 50mm mounted slide
- Nonstop scanning—50 slides at a time

- 48-bit, 5000 DPI
- Magic touch dust and scratch removal (PowerSlide 5000, 2015)

SlideSnap Pro/Lite (Batch Scanner)—$3,395.00/$2,695.00

(Does not include cost of camera)
The SlideSnap scanners work a little differently. They are projectors, built as part of a rig that mounts a DSLR, that "scans" each image at a faster rate than traditional scanners. The catch is, even at a higher price, it does not come with a camera. If your library already has a DSLR that supports wired shutter release, you can use it with these scanners.

The pro can scan 30 slides a minute, and the lite, 15 slides a minute, at a resolution dependent on the camera you have. They are built with vintage Kodak projectors, so they are a mix of old and new components, but built professionally.

- Built on vintage Kodak projects
- Supply your own DSLR
- Resolution dependent on camera
- Fast scan rate
- Up to 140 slides in each batch (SlideSnap Pro, 2015)

(Book Scanner) BinderMinder

One product worth looking into for this need is the BinderMinder. Rather than purchasing a whole new scanner, BinderMinder makes it easy to use existing equipment to digitize book bound materials in a way that treats the book properly.

The BinderMinder uses a cantilevered hinge that lets the copier cover lie flat on a book, rather than the shallower hinge of a traditional copier cover that can put unnecessary pressure on a book's cover and end up damaging it. *Binderminder.com* has additional details and purchasing information. (BinderMinder, 2015)

(Book Scanner) ScanSnap SV600—$795

For those familiar with Fujitsu's ScanSnap family, there is now a book scanning option. With a vertical orientation, this one looks quite a bit different, but offers the ability to scan books, magazines, loose pages, and even 3D objects up to 30mm in height. For documents, it will scan items up to A3 size.

It will automatically adjust for the angle and curves of spreads, and includes OCR. It even auto-detects when you flip the pages and will initiate scanning for each spread or page.

For the ability to scan books, as well as objects and other loose pages, it is fairly affordable. The included software works on both Mac and PC platforms.

- Scans bound material and flat documents
- Scans an A3 size area in less than three seconds
- Book curve image-flattening technology
- Auto crop, de-skew, and rotation features
- Auto page-turn detection sensor
- Searchable PDF, PDF and JPEG creation (ScanSnap SV600, 2015)

DIY Book Scanner

Just as there are DIY methods for digitizing motion pictures and slide, there are options for making your own book scanner as well.

Diybookscanner.org is a website dedicated to showcasing methods for building your own book scanners. Some are as simple as using a digital camera and a piece of glass, others come as kits. They offer instructions for several different methods, most of which involve aiming your camera at a book, on a special rig, and using their free software to process the image and even perform OCR.

They have plenty of resources for getting started, including a forum and a Wiki for answering all your questions.

Carousel Scanner

The Carousel Scanner is a DIY method of "scanning" large quantities of slides in a short amount of time. Scanning is in quotes, because it is not digitizing the image in the same way traditional scanners do.

This is a way of building your own SlideSnap, but with less automation and polish. Essentially, it is a rig that mounts a DSLR camera in front of a carousel projector. With a few modifications, the camera shoots an image of the slides projected into its lens. This way, a slide can be digitized a mere instant after it drops into the projector, and quickly shuffled on to the next one.

With about 10–15 minutes of setup, this method can sift through a 120 slide carousel in a matter of minutes. There are certainly tradeoffs, but it can be the right solution for certain people.

Analog to Digital Converters

Aside from static images, scanners do not do us much good. That is where analog to digital converters (A/D converters) comes in. These are used for taking the signal from time-based media, like audio and video, and converting it to a digital signal so a computer can record the data as a file.

Scanning is an easier place to begin your digitization process, since it is not a linear, time-based process. Digitizing video and audio are. Photos, documents, and other static images are easily digitized within a few seconds, but video and audio are a bit more involved.

Some of these converters are stand-alone units, while others are built into the equipment and players themselves. While scanners mostly rely on USB connections, audio and video equipment will also rely on USB, but also other connections such as FireWire, USB 3.0, and Thunderbolt.

Video

This section mainly addresses video formats that came about in the 1970s and 1980s and were available to the general consumer crowd.

The thing to note about video (and audio) is that when you are digitizing, the process happens in real time. This means that the duration of the actual digitization process will be as long as the duration of the media you are working with. So, a 20-minute VHS tape will take 20 minutes to convert. There is no way to speed up or slow down the process. Of course, you will have to take other things into consideration, like the additional time it takes to finalize a DVD, or to copy a digital video file from one drive to another.

It is important to set this expectation when working with a patron on a project. While digitizing a tape, making a quick edit and burning to DVD may sound like a straightforward process, a lot of time may be required. First, you have the time required to digitize the video, say an hour, for an hour long tape. Once it has been digitized, you might drop it into video editing software, make a few cuts, and add a title. To burn this to DVD, the video has to be converted to a video format specific to DVD. For an hour long video, this can take another 30–90 minutes depending on the power of your computer, plus an additional 10–15 minutes to burn it to a DVD.

The most common format you will encounter is VHS. These were prevalent during the 1980s, and many people have already transferred their films to VHS, and may want to again transfer from VHS to DVD or digital video file.

Other consumer level formats include VHS-C, 8mm, Hi8, Digital8, and MiniDV. If you encounter another format, such as laser disc or Betamax, you can usually accommodate them if they have a working player that you can connect to your A/D converter.

Video Capture Recommendations

This list is by no means exhaustive, but serves as a way to begin your search for scanning equipment.

Grass Valley ADVC-110—$179.99

One of the most affordable and straightforward units for video and audio digitization is the Canopus ADVC-110. However, it requires a FireWire 400 connection, which was prevalent on Macs for about a decade, but is no longer included on new models. There are adapters available for FireWire 400 to FireWire 800 and Thunderbolt.

The ADVC-110 is a small, white unit with a red, white, and yellow composite connection on the front. You will recognize these connections if you have ever hooked up a VCR, DVD player, or game console before. Specifically, before HDMI became a widespread connection.

Any device that has an output that can be connected to the composite connection can be digitized. This can be video and audio, or either one separately. The red and white connections are for audio, left and right. If the source is a mono signal, then it goes into the left channel. The yellow connection is for video.

You could use this unit to digitize the video from a VHS unit, or even just the audio from a reel-to-reel audio player. This can easily be the centerpiece of your video and audio digitization setup. As I mentioned earlier, some patrons may come in with more obscure formats, such as Beta. If the patron has a working Beta player, it can simply be connected to the ADVC-110 and digitized from there.

- Connects analog video to all A/D devices
- Powered by FireWire 400
- Composite (RCA), S-Video I/O
- PC/Mac compatible (ADVC-110, 2015)

Toshiba DVR620 DVD/VHS Recorder—$219.99

This unit is the bread and butter of the video digitization setup we have at the Studio at AHML. It is an all-in-one VHS/DVD combo unit that lets you digitize VHS tapes directly to DVD.

Even though DVDs are a format losing relevance, many people still want that tangible product, thus being so popular. It is also the quickest way to digitize, since it eliminated steps needed when working with files on a computer, like converting between formats more than once and large file transfers.

In addition to converting straight to DVD, this unit offers the ability to record video from multiple sources, including recording outside cameras and other playback devices straight to DVD. It also includes basic titling and menu options. While it has a few quirks (like any equipment), it has proven reliable and relatively easy to use. It has recently been discontinued, but is easily found on Amazon and eBay.

- HDMI output
- Front-panel DV input
- Component video output
- Bi-directional dubbing (Toshiba DVR620, 2105)

Blackmagic Design Intensity Shuttle—$189.05

This unit offers a more compatible connection with USB 3.0 (as well as the even faster Thunderbolt), which offers a greater chance of it working with your Windows computer.

In addition to the composite connections, it also features component and HDMI capture abilities. It also works with many existing video-editing applications, such as Premiere Pro and After Effects. It does not work with Dell computers.

- HD/SD capture/playback
- USB 3.0 support
- Separate sides for inputs and outputs
- Support for multiple video standards
- No separate power source required
- Compatible with multiple applications (Intensity Shuttle, 2015)

Audio

Similar to video, audio also transfers in real time. Luckily, audio is not as resource intensive once it is digitized, so transferring files and converting between different digital formats does not take as long as video. The formats you will most likely encounter are cassette tapes or vinyl records.

There are standalone devices for digitizing audio, often called an audio interface. These are like the A/D converters for video, but specialized for audio. In reality, these are just glorified sound cards (the part of your computer that processes sound both in and out) with higher quality electrical components, additional inputs and outputs, and other routing controls.

Most interfaces connect to your computer via USB (though for awhile, many were FireWire). They often include their own software, though many of the common audio recording and editing apps mentioned later are more than enough for your average digitization needs.

With an interface, you will need to connect the outputs from your playback device to the inputs on the interface. This may require a few adapters or different cables.

There is also a new breed of playback equipment on the market that has the digitization capabilities built in. Essentially, there is an A/D converter built into the cassette deck or the turntable, and the signal outputs via USB, which makes for an easy connection to a computer. Rather than having to select specific inputs on your recording software, you simply select the device, and the rest is taken care of.

Lastly, there are all-in-one units that contain both a cassette deck (or other inputs) and a CD burner that will allow you to directly digitize your audio to a CD, or in some cases, a flash drive.

Audio Recommendations

This list is by no means exhaustive, but serves as a way to begin your search for audio equipment.

The Grass Valley ADVC-110, already mentioned earlier in video recommendations, will also work great as a way to digitize audio from already existing playback devices.

ION Audio Tape 2 PC—$119

This unit operates like your traditional cassette deck, but has an A/D converter built in, which outputs to a USB connection. Once selected as in input on your recording program of choice, you press play on the deck and can begin recording straight to the computer. This is about as straightforward as it gets for digitizing cassette tapes.

- Included EZ vinyl/tape converter creates MP3s
- Dual-dubbing cassette decks for tape-to-tape conversion
- Works with metal and chrome cassette tapes (Tape 2 PC, 2015)

NuMark TTUSB—$139

Just like the Tape 2 PC, the TTUSB does the same thing, but for vinyl records. With an A/D converter built in, this will digitize your records straight to your computer's audio recording software, and otherwise operates like a traditional turntable.

- Adjustable anti-skate control for increased stereo balancing
- 33 1/3 and 45 RPM speed playback
- Line level RCA outputs with built-in preamp
- Adjustable pitch control ±10 percent
- 1/8" stereo line input, RCA line outputs
- USB computer connectivity for PC and Mac
- Included EZ vinyl/tape converter software quickly rips your vinyl collection directly to iTunes (TTUSB, 2015)

M-Audio M-Track—$136

This is a small and affordable recording interface for your computer. It connects via USB and will work with most recording software. In addition to inputs for devices like cassette decks and turntables, it also has two XLR connections for microphones and other pro-audio equipment. This gives you more granularity in terms of controls.

- Two XLR mic inputs with selectable phantom power
- Two balanced 1/4" line inputs with guitar-level switching
- Two TRS 1/4" inserts; one per input channel
- MIDI In and Out jacks
- Balanced 1/4" main outputs with level control
- Headphone out with independent level control (M-Track, 2015)

TASCAM CC-222MKIV—$399.99

This is an all-in-one unit that operates without the need for a computer or software. With a built in cassette deck and a CD burner, it can digitize tape directly to CD.

It has additional inputs on the back for recording from other devices straight to CD as well. This eliminates the need for a computer and learning any accompanying software.

- RCA analog unbalanced inputs/outputs
- Pitch and speed can be varied
- Auto space function that inserts about four seconds of silence between tracks during playback
- Sync recording function that automatically starts recording when sound begins
- Automatic track division: automatically insert a track division at a preset condition
- Independent input and output are possible for the CD and cassette sections
- Dubbing is possible both ways between the CD and cassette sections (CC222MIKV, 2015)

Motion Pictures

While photos and tapes will probably be the bulk of what patrons bring in to digitize, many of them will have older formats, such as motion pictures in 8mm, Super 8mm, and 16mm formats. These formats present unique challenges.

Chances are, if you have ever talked to a patron about digitization, they have requested the ability to work with 8mm, Super 8mm, or 16mm film. Chances are, you also had to turn them away since those facilities are difficult to offer.

In recent years, there have been a handful of items on the market that begin to approach affordability. For many years, the only real options were the DIY methods mentioned earlier. While those are great for access copies or as fun projects, they do not do the original film justice.

Because of their age, many of the films have begun to decay, often becoming brittle and difficult to work with. The projectors used to play them back are also hard to find in good, working order. You may luck out on places like eBay and Craigslist for used projectors, but in my experience, even projectors in good condition will work for a few months at best before giving problems. Once issues arise, finding someone to repair them is difficult, especially if you do not live near a large metro area.

However, there are methods for digitizing that are still somewhat accessible. While the professional options are more expensive, there are DIY ways to go about it.

Motion Picture Recommendations

This list is by no means exhaustive, but serves as a way to begin your search for motion picture equipment.

RetroScan Universal—$4,500

The RetroScan Universal is a brand new, handmade film digitization unit. This is unique, since many companies use vintage projectors, constantly maintained for operation, to digitize film.

These units are made from new parts, and operate in safer and more reliable ways than older equipment. They are made by a small company out of Texas, MovieStuff LLC that specializes in this equipment.

When purchasing this unit, you have the option of ordering multiple gates. Each gate is made to work with a specific film type. For example, one type will work with both 8mm and Super8, called a dual 8 gate. You would need a separate gate for 16mm. One gate is included in the purchase price, and each additional gate is $500.

The unit performs true frame-by-frame digitization as well, scanning each frame individually as it passes under the camera. Each frame is saved as an individual photo file. There are also no sprockets or pinch rollers, resulting in a safer movement of film through the unit. The software (an additional $199.95) allows you to compress the image files into different video or photo formats.

On top of that, it offers manual exposure and color controls as well. More details can be found at *moviestuff.tv*. If you are able to round up the funding, possibly through a grant, book sales, or elsewhere, this would be a great addition to any digitization program.

Many services charge upward of $30–$40 per film for digitization, so in the long term, this may prove to be a good investment for your patrons.

- Output 1080p HD, 720p HD or SD files
- No sprockets, no claws, no pinch rollers
- True, codec free frame-by-frame scanning
- Regular 8, Super 8, 9.5mm, 16mm on same unit
- Scan compressed or uncompressed
- Adjustable cropping for maximum image area (RetroScan, 2015)

DIY Method

If a professional unit is out of reach, or the demand is not there to justify a higher price point, there are DIY methods.

First, there is the off-the-wall method. Essentially, this involves projecting the film (a working projector is required) onto a wall, or other projection surface. From there, you position a digital camera slightly off axis (right next to, above, or below the projector) and shoot the projected image.

The second method, although similar, is slightly different. In this case, the image is projected into a telecine box. This box has a mirror inside, angled to reflect the projected image out a window on the side. On the side is a mount for a digital camera that records the reflected image.

In each case, the result is a digital video file on the camera. While this method may work in some cases, the clarity, quality and overall experience don't come close to purchasing professional equipment. There are a range of issues from flicker and focus to exposure that you'll encounter with the DIY methods.

Computers

While the equipment we have covered so far is all important, computers are still the lynchpin that make most of these processes work. The scanners, A/D converters, and other gear all connect to a computer. Specifically, it is the software we use with these tools that allow us to really work with them.

There is a good chance that if your library has any computers available, you will not have to purchase a new machine. As with any other equipment, when you purchase a computer, make sure it has the recommended specs necessary to operate with your equipment.

Mac or PC

While this was once a much more relevant debate, the choice between a Mac or PC is not as crucial anymore. Your main concern here is the software that you will be using with each piece of equipment. That may do the choosing for you. For example, if the software that comes with a certain piece of gear runs only on Windows, then you know you will be working with PCs.

This debate may also be settled when you begin working with your IT staff. They may recommend one platform over another depending on the library's current tech.

You may not need to purchase a new computer though. Your library may have an extra one available for use. As long as its specifications are up to snuff (not a very hard test to pass with some digitization equipment), you can most likely use it for scanning.

Digitizing photos and audio do not require much processing power, but working with the digitized video files does. Keep in mind that video is the most intensive medium to work with. While an older computer may digitize the video just fine, editing it or rendering to a different format will take much longer with an aging computer.

Also consider what other organizations in your community work with. For example, in my library's community, the local school district is equipped with Macs. Because our scanning equipment is part of our digital media lab, which serves a variety of purposes outside of digitization, we went with Macs so that children and parents coming in to use our lab can use the same software and equipment they use at school. This is not a necessity, and may not be viable with your given budget, but it is worth considering how it all ties into the community on a greater level.

Recommendations

For computers, I will not be recommending specific models since the configurability is endless, and the decision may be influenced by factors such as your IT staff, established vendors, and other purchasing policies your library may have.

The great thing about digitization for the average person is that it does not require top of the line equipment or powerhouse computers.

While a fast machine will result in a smoother and quicker process overall, your average computer can handle the stresses of digitization just fine. The following are some baseline specifications recommended for scanning photos, documents, slides, and film negatives. This applies to audio and video as well.

- Windows 7 or newer
- Mac OS X 10.6 or newer
- 2 GHz processor or faster
- 2GB RAM (4GB recommended)

If you would like to work on editing or restoration of the materials, the aforementioned specs for a computer will get the job done, but editing, rendering, and working with audio and video are more resource intensive, and the following specification would provide you a better overall experience with these more advanced steps.

- Windows 7 or newer
- Mac OS X 10.6 or newer
- 3 GHz processor or faster
- 8GB RAM (4GB recommended)

Some software may also require newer version of Windows or Mac OS X to run. Again, your IT staff would be a great source to start determining the exact specs of the computer(s) you purchase.

Scanning is the lightest activity in terms of the power needed. Chances are, whatever computer you end up using, even if it has been in use for five or more years, will be able to handle scanning just fine.

The next step up in power is audio. Audio files, if over a few minutes, tend to be larger than photos. If you are converting between formats, the processing power of the computer requires more resources. This is most important when processing large audio files. Think 30 minutes to several hours long.

The most resource intensive media is video. Since video is essentially a sequence of images played rapidly, you are dealing with potentially tens of thousands to even hundreds of thousands of photos for any given video depending on its length.

Not only does digitizing video happen in real time, but saving and compressing that captured video to a file also requires more time. This is dependent on the speed of your computer's CPU. Then if the result is a large HD video file, maybe 10GB or more, this can take a lot of time to transfer to your storage device, depending on the connection and transfer speed afforded by the computer and storage device.

Software

Software is the main tool you will be working with to achieve your digitization goals. While the scanner and computer are obviously important, the software is the part you will mostly be interacting.

While each piece of software is different, they all generally offer the same core functionality, and for the most part, this is all you will need.

Native

Windows and Mac OS X both come with native, meaning built-in, solutions to scanning. In Windows, it is called Windows Fax and Scan, on the Mac, it is called Image Capture. These are free, built-in apps that provide no frills, basic scanning functionality, but may prove to be all you need.

Third Party

There are also third-party programs that provide additional flexibility, such as more image format options, better correctional tools, and more power overall. Names include Silverfast and VueScan.

Most scanners you purchase come with their own software. Whatever software it comes with usually does the job. For example, the Epson scanners come with EpsonScan, software developed by Epson to accompany its scanners.

While all the programs may look different, for the most part, they all provide the same functionality. As long as you can scan and crop your photos, adjust settings like DPI, bit depth and file format, you are generally good to go.

Some software features things like the ability to scan more than one image at once, color correction settings, dust and scratch removal and more.

Editing

Lastly, software that aids you in restoring, correcting, or fixing your digitized files is worth looking at. For examples, many of these programs allow you to fix scratches and tears on photos, clicks and pops in audio, and color on video.

Photoshop is probably the most well-known software for fixing photos and documents. Just because it is the industry standard, it does not mean that it is the right choice. There are other simple, sometimes native solutions to media correction that are worth looking into. For example, the Photos app on Macs allows you to do some basic image corrections, cropping, and other adjustments, all at no additional charge or hassle.

For audio, there is a free program called Audacity. This works on both Macs and PCs, and allows you to split and crop audio, add effects, remove hiss and pop, and even tweak things like the frequency range with Equalization (EQ).

Some scanning software comes with built in correctional functions. For example, EpsonScan comes with dust removal features.

Recommendations

Usually, any scanner you purchase comes with its own software. Because of the wide variety, I cannot discuss each piece of software, but generally, they all include the same basic features. As long as you can choose DPI, bit depth, photo format, and a handful of other features, you should be good. The user experience with each software title will be different, so it is a matter of what you think provides the best experience and capability overall.

Scanning software worth looking into includes Silverfast and VueScan. For audio, Audacity, Reaper, Garageband, Logic Pro, and Pro Tools may be good options. For video, iMovie, Final Cut, Premiere Pro, and Windows Movie Maker may suit your needs. Lastly, for photos, look into Photoshop, GIMP, or Pixelmator.

Warranties

As with any large equipment purchase, you will want to take a look at return policies and warranties. A one-year warranty should be the minimum, and make sure to look at reviews and other people's experience with the manufacturer's repair and warranty support. With the public using the equipment, good coverage and repair are that much more important.

Storage

It is extremely important to consider your storage options when digitizing files. In fact, this should be decided upon before you even begin the process of converting your materials.

One of the main reasons we digitize to begin with is to store our memories in a different form. While the physical version of our materials is tangible and real, they are prone to physical wear and tear. Digitizing them before this happens, lets us keep a copy of our memories in a state of better condition.

Hard Drives

The most common method for storing your files is on external hard drive. This is different than the internal hard drive on your computer.

Often times, digitizing large amounts of material takes up an equally large amount of space. It is not always convenient to house digitized files on your main internal hard drive. External hard drives provide ample storage, but keep your digitized files separate from the everyday files that get used on your computer. By keeping your main hard drive lean, you will lessen the risk of slowing down the computer.

You can get one terabyte (TB) of storage for under $100 nowadays, which is more than enough space for the average patron. One TB of space can hold approximately one million photos, depending on the settings put in place when scanning.

Optical Storage

People who learned to use a computer in the late 1990s or early millennium are most likely familiar and comfortable with CDs and DVDs as a storage medium. While they are quickly going out of fashion, and not as convenient as hard drives (and flash drives), they are a valid backup medium.

CDs hold about 700MB of data, while DVDs hold 4.7GB. These formats may be harder to access in the future (who will have a readily available CD/DVD reader in 10–15 years?), but making a copy of your files to these discs can prove to be a handy alternative. Think of these as copies that are seldom accessed, and stored away, but always there if need be.

Included in optical storage is also the newer Blu-Ray format. These hold anywhere from 25–50GB, and have the same general benefits and drawbacks as CDs and DVDs.

Flash Drives

Flash drives are probably the most convenient method for storing your files. Flash storage is affordable, convenient, and universal. Some people also know of these as thumb drives or jump drives. These are not to be confused with Zip drives, which were popular at the turn of the millennium, but generally unavailable at this point.

Flash drives range in size from under 1GB to 1TB, and most people have one sitting in their purse or connected to their keychain.

They are easy to connect to any USB port, and quickly show up on the computer for use. In terms of convenience, these win out. They are slower to read and write than external hard drives, but some offer USB 3.0 transfer speeds, which are very quick.

Cloud

Another convenient method of storing your digitized files is cloud storage. This is storage on the Internet, so that you can access your files wherever you have an Internet connection. Many services, such as Dropbox, Google Drive, and iCloud give you a specified amount of space for free, and allow for larger allowances for a fee.

Cloud storage is great as another method of backup. It is also a quick and easy way to share your photos or documents with friends and family. The cloud eliminates the need to physically have a storage device to view the materials, since the Internet itself is the storage device.

This method also takes the maintenance and technical responsibility off the user's plate. Cloud services have professional engineers and technicians working to maintain and support the infrastructure. The only thing the user needs to worry about is managing his or her files and assets. The rest is taken care of.

There is no perfect solution for storage. Each medium has its own advantages and drawbacks. Hard drives crash, flash drives are lost, cloud services are hacked, and companies go under. The best thing to keep in mind is redundancy. Keep your data backed up in multiple locations, and on various forms of media. This provides you the best chance of keeping your memories safe and far from any sort of data disaster.

Drive Formats

In working with customers, you are going to get involved in saving their files to a flash drive or external hard drive. Given the wide range of brands, and the variety of computers any given patron will have, you will want to be familiar with the common formats out there that any given storage device depends on.

These formats are different than file formats, such as JPEG or MP3. Drive formats provide the underlying structure of a disk so a computer can read, write, and work with files. Having the correct format will determine which platforms the drive will work with, what file sizes you can work with, and in special cases, which software will work with the drive.

Most drives are formatted to work with Windows. So much so, that for the most part, a drive's packaging will specifically call out that it is formatted for a Mac, otherwise, you can assume it is for Windows. Formats are not permanent, and can be easily changed from any computer.

Of course, when erasing, or formatting a drive, you will lose all of its data. If there is anything important on the disk worth keeping, you will need to copy it to the computer first, and then restore the data to the drive once the format is complete. Here are the most common formats you are likely to encounter when working with patrons.

NTFS

NTFS is the default file system for Windows, starting with Windows Vista back in 2007. Any drive formatted with this structure can be both written to and read from a Windows machine. There are no limits to file size or drive size that would be of any concern at this point in time.

However, without special software, a Mac can only read from an NTFS drive. It cannot write new files or make changes to existing files on an NTFS drive. It will recognize only the drive and allow you to access its files.

If there is any possibility a patron may want to share his or her files with a Mac using his or her flash drive or external hard drive, NTFS will not be an option he or she can work with.

HFS+ (Mac OS Journaled)

HFS+ is the file system that Mac computers rely on. Unlike NTFS, it can niether be written to or read from a Windows machine. It will be useful only for patrons who rely solely on Macs.

It also provides ample accommodation for large file sizes and drive sizes. There are no limits to file size or drive size that would be of any concern at this point.

FAT32

This format is probably the most common format you will encounter for external hard drives and flash drives. This is because it is both read- and write-friendly from Windows and Mac computers. It has been around for over 20 years, and has proven reliable.

The main drawback, since it is an aging format from a time when file sizes and drive sizes were much smaller, is that it cannot work with files over 4GB, or drives larger than 2TB. Now, with HD video, you are likely to encounter files much larger than 4GB, so FAT32 will not be a good option for video projects. While a 2TB is not rare, at this point, most people still will not be carrying around drives that large, especially flash drives.

exFAT

Finally, this format provides the greatest flexibility and is often the best choice as a format for a patron's flash drive or external hard drive. Like FAT32, it can be both read from and written to Windows and Mac machines. Unlike FAT32 though, it has no file size or drive size limit that would be of concern to today's storage needs.

How Can I Tell the Format of a Drive?

Figuring out the format of your drive is relatively straightforward. First, plug your drive into the computer, and give it a minute to be recognized.

For Windows, go to My Computer. A window will appear, listing all the drives connected to the computer. Right click on the flash drive or external hard drive, and select *Properties*. This window will display some information about the drive, including its format.

For Mac, click on the Finder icon on the dock. In the window that appears, your drive will show up on the left side, under devices. Usually, a new drive is called Untitled, or often bears the name of the manufacturer of the drive.

Ctrl-click (or right click if enabled) on the drive, and select *Get Info*. A small window will appear, and toward the top will be the drive's basic information, including its format.

How Do I Change the Format of a Drive?

Remember that formatting a drive will erase all data, unless you copy your files to another drive, or your computer, first.

To change the format of a drive on Windows, open up My Computer, as stated earlier. Right click on the drive, and select Format. From the window that pops up, choose a format from the drop-down menu, then click format.

On the Mac, open up Disk Utility, which can be found under *Applications > Utilities > Disk Utility*. Choose your drive in the left hand pane, and choose the Erase tab at the top of the window. From there, choose your format from the drop-down menu, and click erase.

Chapter 5

The Digitization Process

PREPARATION

Now for the actual digitization process. This can vary based on the equipment you have purchased or have on hand, but this chapters aims to outline general guidelines, terminology, and methods that are applicable to all pieces of equipment.

You will need to reference the instructions that were provided with your equipment, but the workflow is generally the same across different devices. Even though software has quite a bit of variation, there are similar settings and options throughout most of them.

Plan out your process. Decide what materials are to be digitized, how you would like to organize them, what formats you want them in, and where you want to display the final result, or where the data will be stored and backed up.

Prepare your materials and the equipment by properly cleaning them before use. Brush off any dust or oils that may diminish the quality of the digitized file. Once your materials are in place to be digitized, pull up your software and set properties like the DPI, format, quality options, destination, and others.

Now that everything is set up, let the digitization begin. With your assets digitized, make sure your files are properly named and organized. Once everything is in place, we want to store our files for easy access, and back them up in multiple forms and places.

Setting Up the Equipment

While it is always exciting to receive your new equipment, you will want to be patient in getting everything set up and working properly.

Take some time to open the packaging slowly to make sure all the materials are in good condition and intact in case you need to send anything back. Do not throw away the packaging until you have tested everything and know it is working well.

Look through the manual and get familiar with the equipment's ins and outs. The last thing you want to do is rush into setting up the equipment, only to break something or treat the equipment poorly.

Do several tests on some trial materials, something you do not mind damaging, to make sure the equipment is in good, working order. Make sure to run it through the paces, with various materials, different settings, and different situations that users might put it through. This will help you discover the quirks and nuances of the equipment and software.

Once you feel confident running the equipment and are sure everything is working, you can begin to think about letting the public use it.

Organize Materials

Part of preparation includes getting your materials ready and organized. This could mean splitting photos into different events or organized by a specific person or place.

If the patron contributes materials to your library for display or to a local history collection, work with him or her to select and curate the materials that best suit that specific project. If you have a large collection of media to digitize, you will want to get everything in order. What types of media will be digitized? Is all the equipment working and ready to go? What is the most important media? Where do I store it?

These are all questions you will want to answer before beginning the process. Many people have large collections of materials to sift through, and it is important to go through everything!

Chances are that not everything in those old storage boxes is gold. If there are photos that are out of focus, do not provide you any value or connection, or just bad photos, there is no need to digitize them. Since you are spending time and possibly some money on these projects, make sure you do it efficiently, and that means digitizing what is of actual value to you or a local history collection, and knowing what is not worth it. There is a temptation to digitize every piece of history you might have, but it is often not the case that everything is worth holding on to.

Cleaning Originals

Chances are that your materials have been sitting in a box or other container, likely in your basement or other dark place. By the time you have dug up your materials, you realize that they are not in the best condition. This is all part of the process.

In digging through your original materials, you may find some of the photos have been discolored, have rotted, or that your motion pictures are brittle. While you will ideally want the cleanest materials possible to digitize for best results, it may not be the right solution. Luckily, there are a few things you can do before and after digitization to clean up your results.

With no experience in cleaning old media, and without the knowledge of different emulsion types, the chemicals involved, and other important information, attempting to clean your materials may just make things worse.

Some experts suggest digitizing the damaged media first and using digital tools to correct flaws. This way, you will not damage the original further, and will be able to have a nice, high-quality, digital, corrected version.

Of course, if you are in doubt, contact a professional. The last thing you would want to do is make things worse, so it is likely worth it to seek out experienced, professional help to make sure your media gets the proper treatment. If you are curious about cleaning items yourself, here are a few basic guidelines and tips.

Photos

There are a few things you can do to prepare your photos for scanning, depending on what condition they are in.

First, make sure to have some white cotton gloves on. This will prevent you from making things worse. A soft brush and canned air will be your first options for cleaning your photos. Use these to remove any dirt or dust. If there is a more difficult layer of dust or dirt, make sure to be very careful, as you do not want to damage the photo. Remember, if you cannot fix the issue without damaging the photo, scan it anyway and attempt to correct it later using software like Photoshop.

For negatives, the same goes for the white cotton gloves, a soft brush, and the canned air. There are also lint-free film clothes you can purchase to safely clean the film. Lastly, isopropyl alcohol can be gently wiped across the negatives to remove further residue. Always test on an unimportant photo to make sure no damage occurs. Never use water on the emulsion side either. It can cause permanent damage.

You may also try PEC-Pads or PEC-12 solution for cleaning most film and print emulsions. They can also be used for cleaning scanners, CDs, mirrors, lenses, and other optical equipment.

Specific details on when and when not to use these items can be found at http://www.cameraclean.co.uk/PEC-12.php.

Video

For VHS tapes, there are cleaning units that clean the tape heads on the player itself. This does not fix the tape, but cleans the heads in the VHS unit, ensuring better playback and treatment of tapes.

To clean the VHS player itself, there are very easy-to-use cleaning kits available. Most of these entail a fake VHS tape with a strip of cloth inside instead of tape. You place a few drops of cleaning solution onto the cloth strip, then run it through your VCR for a minute or so, and the play heads inside the unit are cleaned.

Luckily, most tape-based media since the advent of VHS and Betamax have held up pretty well. However, they are still prone to issues, such as mold and moisture.

Audio

Depending on how audio was stored, and in which format it is in, its condition can vary quite a bit. For example, 1/4 inch tape reels may be rotting and decaying if they were stored in a dark and moist place, most likely in a basement. Remember to bring items to a professional if you are not confident in your ability to clean the media.

For cassette tapes, you can use a microfiber cleaning cloth to gently press down on the tape while you wind it through with a pencil. This will remove dust and other debris for better playback.

For vinyl records, you can use a soft, lint-free cloth to remove dust, distilled water for a bit of a deeper clean, or a 20 percent isopropyl alcohol solution for a more detailed clean. Do your best to avoid getting the record's label wet.

Motion Pictures

You can wind your film slowly through a projector's take-up reel while using a soft, lint-free cloth to remove dust and other debris. For specific frame, you can spot-clean them with a cotton swab dampened with film cleaner.

Digitized Copies

Before you begin the digitization process, it is important to understand the difference between preservation copies and access copies. Depending on the individuals' need, some people may only need preservation copies, but having version that are easy to access for reference can be convenient and helpful as well.

Access Copies

Access copies, as they are named, serve the purpose of easy access and convenience. These are lower-quality, fast-loading copies of your digitized files that are simple to access and reference. These could be for getting a grasp of your collection, quickly looking at a handful of pictures, or for quickly sharing with friends and family.

In general, access copies are characterized by a reduced sampling rate (audio), lower bitrate (audio and video), and are fairly compressed (all formats).

Preservation Copies

Preservation copies, on the other hand, can be either the original document or a high-quality, uncompressed digitized copy of the original, to serve as the master source for subsequent copies. Because they are the master source, they should be seldom accessed as to keep down wear and tear, possible damage, accidental deletion, or other possible accidents. They are generally high-quality, uncompressed, versions of the original.

The Environment

The first step in working with clean materials is to work in an area that is as free of dust and dirt as possible. Keep this in mind when developing a space for these digitization projects. If you can, avoid windows, vents, and fans. Do your best to avoid placing the scanner on any sort of fabric as well, since this builds up static electricity. I realize this is not entirely practical, especially when working with an existing space, but do your best and use common sense.

THE SCANNING PROCESS

Now that we have a grasp on the equipment, it is time to dive into the actual process of digitization. In the following sections, we will discuss the specific properties, formats, and other information you will need to know for ending up with some well-digitized materials.

DPI/PPI

PPI, or pixels per inch, is the resolution at which a material is scanned at. A pixel is the basic building block of digital screens, or the tiny squares that make up a digital image. The higher the PPI, the finer the detail will be captured on the image. Pixel is an abbreviation for picture element.

DPI, or dots per inch, is the resolution at which an image is printed. Printers drop tiny dots of ink on a page to form an image. Just like PPI, the higher the DPI, the great the detail of an image will be printed.

While these terms are technically different, scanning manufacturers often use the terms interchangeably. Because this book focuses on digitization and not printing, both terms pertain to the pixels per inch. I will use DPI throughout the book since it is commonly used.

It is important to note that this does not necessarily mean higher quality. As the saying goes, "Garbage in, garbage out." If the quality of the original copy is not good, the digitized copy is not going to be any better, and this pertains to any material you will digitize. A higher DPI setting will simply mean that all imperfections, as well as the good parts, will show up in greater detail. A high DPI setting also means that any reproductions can be made at a larger size.

For example, if the image you are scanning is out of focus, that is what you are stuck with. Digitizing it will not perform any improvements or enhancements. Things like scratches, dust, color, and exposure can be corrected, but something like focus is permanent.

You have probably run into a low-quality, or low-resolution digital photo, one that looks blocky or blurry, where you can see individual pixels. This is what happens when you scan an image at a given DPI level, and enlarge beyond that.

For example, the standard DPI setting is 300. This is considered native size, meaning that scanning a 4×6 image at 300 DPI will result in a digital copy that is meant to be viewed no larger than 4×6.

If you would like to scan a 4×6 image and view or print it at twice its native size, you would double the DPI to 600, where you could work with it at 8×12, and so on with larger DPI settings. Of course, you may still reach a point where the DPI chosen is beyond the original quality of the photo. This is especially true with prints. Original photographic sources, such as film negatives, however, give you a much higher range of quality to play with.

A higher DPI setting will also result in a larger file size and a longer scan time. These are the options you will have to keep in mind when allotting the time you have available to give to any digitization project, as well as how much storage space you have.

For a little perspective, on an average flatbed scanner, once all settings are dialed in, it may take 10 seconds to scan a 4×6 image at 300 DPI. The resulting file size would be roughly 300KB as a JPEG format. Formats will be explained in the next section.

When you hear of miracles happening in the digital world, it is usually in postproduction, most likely in Photoshop, where after some time and effort is spent, glaring flaws can be fixed. The digitization process itself aims to create as close a reproduction as possible of the original. This includes dust, scratches, tears, and other imperfections.

Some scanning software has built-in capabilities to address flaws during the digitization process. Epson Scan, for example, has automatic dust removal, and a technology called Digital Ice removes scratches and other imperfections.

However, with anything automatic, it does not always work correctly. It sometimes leaves visual artifacts, making it obvious that something was removed, and does not look convincing or natural. These features also results in a longer scan time.

Bit Depth

Bit depth refers to the amount of unique colors an image can display. For example, a 1 bit image can display only two colors, while a 24 bit image can display over 16 million colors, often referred to as true color.

The human eye can detect around 10 million colors, so 24 bit covers the gamut. Plus, the added range allows photos to hold up better under editing and post-processing.

It is standard to digitize items at least at 16 bit (around 65,000 colors). That said, there is not much reason not to use 24 bit, unless you are looking to save on file size, or the document is black and white.

Formats

Just like all forms of media we will be dealing with, images have several different formats to choose from, each serving a different purpose dependent on the end goal and the specific document being digitized.

The main formats we will be dealing with are JPEG, TIFF, PDF, GIF, and PNG. Each format has its advantages and disadvantages, all of which will be outlined next.

JPEG

JPEG is the most universal image format. Unless you have a higher-end digital camera, chances are that most digital photos you have taken and most photos you have seen on the web or received in your e-mail are JPEGs.

There are a few reasons why it is such a popular and universal format. The first is that they have a relatively small file size, yet they are still of high enough quality to display as photos in everyday situations.

Their small file size is achieved through compression. Because JPEGs are compressed, they are considered a lossy (as opposed to lossless) format. This compression reduces the file size, but (generally) without crossing into territory where the viewer notices a loss in quality.

Essentially, when you scan an image, the computer temporarily holds that high-quality, lossless image in its memory. When you save as a JPEG, you can choose the amount of compression. Too much compression and the resulting image will have what are known as artifacts, or unnatural looking blocks of color that appear from over-compression. On the bright side, your file size will be small.

The trick here is to walk the line between compression and a manageable file size. Luckily, even a JPEG with minimal compression has a usable file size, maybe just a few megabytes at most for a 4×6 image. Storage space is so affordable now that it hardly ever makes sense to digitize an image at such low quality, or high compression.

Because JPEGs can look good with a relatively small file size, they have become the standard format in for the web. They are convenient for transferring and sending to others.

Oftentimes, JPEG will be your go-to format. Even though there are higher-quality, uncompressed options, for the average user, a JPEG will meet that balance between convenience, file size, and quality.

You can also have different versions of an image. So, you may scan your photos as high-quality, low compression JPEGs, and save more heavily compressed versions for posting on the web or for e-mailing.

TIFF

On the other hand, we have TIFFs. These are uncompressed images with large file sizes. The advantage here is that you do not lose any quality.

Even a minimally compressed JPEG has shed some of the original data from the scan. From the get go, you have lost something. TIFFs retain all quality, but take up much more space; sometimes two to three times as much. Because they are higher quality, they offer better performance for editing. Keep this in mind if you want to edit the photo or document after it has been digitized.

Again, with space so affordable these days, it sometimes makes sense to digitize everything as a TIFF, and save access copies as JPEGs for specific images that you would like to share with others or post online.

This is a personal call. Try scanning a few images as both a JPEG and TIFF and see how you feel about the trade-offs between the two.

Keep in mind that because TIFFs can be such large files, depending on the power of your computer, opening a photo may be slow, especially if you open multiple photos. Not all software will work with TIFFs either, not are they often found on the web. This is not a problem you will run into with JPEGs.

It may be a good idea to scan some of your more prized photos and documents as TIFFs, and the rest as JPEGs. Again, after some experimenting, this is a call you will want to make before proceeding with your entire project.

PDF

PDF, which stands for portable document format, is a highly universal and widely supported format, much like a JPEG. The format itself, though, is much different.

Think of a PDF as a container, and inside that container, you can place all sorts of files, such as JPEGs, TIFFs, Word documents, text, and even audio and video files.

PDF-viewing software allows you to view these contents as long as they are in a PDF format. Because PDFs are great at carrying all sorts of different files, they are great for documents. For example, a company newsletter with text, graphics, and photos will often be saved as a PDF since it is so convenient for transporting all that content.

In terms of digitization, PDFs do best for scanned documents, such as forms, text, or other basic materials. Anything photographic in nature, or even graphical, is best served by the TIFF or JPEG format. From that point, a copy can be saved as a PDF, or multiple photos and documents merged into a PDF for more convenient sharing.

GIF

While not that relevant to digitization, GIFs do have their place. GIFs are great for simple graphics, like logos, charts, and other illustrations. GIFs support only up to 256 colors, and do best for simple graphics, not so much photo-realistic images.

PNG

PNGs are lossless and uncompressed. Their file size is larger than that of a JPEG, especially at high resolutions. PNG's have the best support for transparency within an image.

Scanning File Sizes

Because storage is so affordable these days, TIFFs and high-quality JPEGs are practical format options. Highly compressed JPEGs best serve as copies for the web, or quick-access copies.

Before you begin your project in earnest, as mentioned before, it is wise to have your settings dialed in, so you have consistency and predictability with your storage. If you decide to go with JPEG as a format (which most patrons will likely do), you have options in terms of how compressed your photos will be.

In most apps, when choosing your file settings, there is a quality or compression slider for the JPEG format. The more compression you choose, the smaller the file size will be, but the photo will be of lower quality, with artifacts, inconsistent color grading, and other flaws.

Again, with space being so affordable these days, it is usually not a problem to stick with the highest-quality settings. Even with the highest-quality settings—for example, a quality setting of 100, or the least amount of compression, still results in some compression. JPEGs by nature are lossy, no matter the quality level. If you truly want no compression, and the highest-quality possible, stick with TIFF.

To give you some perspective on the resulting file sizes for different scans, here are the results of digitizing a color 35mm slide, in JPEG and TIFF formats at various DPI levels. The JPEG compression settings were as low as the Epson Scan software goes, meaning minimal compression, for the first JPEG, and for the second JPEG, compression is very high. Notice the differences in file size. These are the trade-offs you will want to keep in mind.

300 DPI

- TIFF-302KB
- JPEG (low compression)-86KB
- JPEG (high compression)- 10KB

600 DPI

- TIFF-1.2MB
- JPEG (low compression)-304KB
- JPEG (high compression)-31KB

1200 DPI

- TIFF-4.7MB
- JPEG (low compression)-1.1MB
- JPEG (high compression)- 110KB

2400 DPI

- TIFF-18.8MB
- JPEG (low compression)-4.3MB
- JPEG (high compression)-356KB

So, for example, if you are trying to determine how much space you would need, you can do some simple math once you have figured out what settings you are going with. For 2,500 slides digitized as TIFFs at a resolution of 2400 DPI, you will need around 47GB (18.8MB × 2,500 slides) of storage. For 1,000 slides scanned as high-quality JPEGs at a resolution of 600 DPI, you would need about 300MB (304KB × 1,000 slides).

Keep in mind these are approximations, since every piece of software may compress JPEGs at slightly different rates.

DIY Batch Scanner

One of the biggest reasons patrons are not always willing to digitize their slide collections is the sheer number of slides they have. I routinely talk to patrons who have collections in the tens of thousands, and the prospect of scanning 4–12 at a time, with a few minutes per batch, is daunting and unexciting.

For some, it works out. They are retired, and decide to come in once or twice a week for a few hours at a time, and over the course of a year or two, their collection is digitized. But that is not realistic or practical for everyone.

With batch scanners sometimes being cost prohibitive, there is a DIY method that may work in your case. It requires some elbow grease and a willingness to dig in. The whole process is a little rough around the edges, but can prove to be an effective solution for some patrons with large slide collections.

I like to refer to it as a carousel scanner, since it directly utilizes a carousel projector. But in reality, it is not a scanner at all, but a modified slide projector and a digital camera. Essentially, you are taking photos of each slide as it is projected into the camera's lens. This allows for very rapid digitization. The quality is not as good as a traditional flatbed scanner, but for many, it passes the test.

I was able to pull this contraption together by finding other people who had done something similar (and honestly, a bit more polished and automated), and had posted instructions and videos online.

Here are a few of the resources I used.

- https://www.youtube.com/watch?v=jnvhBXQrfzQ
- http://www.stockholmviews.com/speedscanner/

First, you will need a slide projector. The more slides it can hold, the quicker you will be able to run through batches of slides. Many Kodak projectors take trays that hold either 80 or 120 slides. When everything is set up, you can run through a tray in a just a few minutes.

A few modifications will need to be done to the projector. First, you will want to remove the lens. It is not needed since we are not projecting it onto a large screen for an audience. Rather, we are just shooting the image straight into the digital camera's lens. It is a good idea to leave the projector's lens housing in place to shield the projected image from outside light.

Second, we will have to modify the light source. The projector's bulb is often too powerful and bright for this, so it needs to be diffused. This can be done by placing some vellum paper in the projector. In Kodak projectors, the bulb projects light through a thick piece of glass. In front of that glass is where you would like to place the vellum. Be careful not to place the vellum between the bulb and the glass itself since the bulb gets extremely hot and you run the risk of burning the paper.

Now you have modified the projector to your needs. The light will be diffused and muted through the vellum, and the projected image will be suitable for the camera without the projector's focusing lens.

Next, you will need a DSLR and a macro lens. For some, you may have this on hand as part of an already existing digital media lab or makerspace. If you do not have this equipment, you may spend between $1,000–$1,500 or more on the camera and lens.

Some batch scanners start at $1,500, so it may not be worth it for you. However, the DSLR is a multipurpose device and can serve other functions as well, so the flexibility may be worth it in your specific situation.

You will want to mount the projector and the DSLR to a common surface. In my case, I made a scrappy wood foundation for both items. The projector fits into a three-sided mount on one end of the wood panel, and the DSLR mounts on to a macro rail attached at the other end. A macro rail allows you to finely adjust the camera's position, both side-to-side and forward and backward. This is important for framing a tight shot of your slides.

The main reason this setup works quickly is the instantaneous nature of both the camera and the projector. The camera shoots in an instant, and the projector can switch between slides quickly. It helps to have the two working together.

The easiest and most cost-effective way is with remotes. Purchase a remote for your DSLR, and a remote for the projector. Once all the settings are dialed in, you can use the remotes to move through the process. Shoot the picture, advance the slide, shoot the picture, advance the slide. Repeat until the tray is finished.

If you are particularly clever, and familiar with circuitry and programming, you can rig up an electrical connection between the camera and the projector. Some folks have used things like an Arduino or Raspberry Pi and a little bit of code to automate the process.

Go ahead and fire up your camera, put it into manual mode, turn on the projector, and drop a slide into the tray. Adjust your aperture, ISO, and shutter speed until the preview looks decent, and take a few minutes to frame up your image correctly. Use the macro rail to finely tune the images position in your frame, and focus on the slide.

You will notice that the perfectly rectangular nature of the camera's frame and the slightly rounded corners of the slide conflict with one another.

There are two ways you can approach this. The first is to include a little bit of the black border in your images. After the fact, you can crop the images to your liking either individually (time consuming) or with a batch crop process in software like Photoshop or Lightroom. There will be some variation since every slide sits slightly differently in the projector.

The second way is to crop ahead of time. You can focus in on the image a little tighter so you exclude the corners and borders. You will lose a little bit of the photo's edges, but your resulting images will be cropped and ready to go.

You will also notice that the images appear backward. This is because rather than viewing them projected onto a screen, the slides are being shot straight into the camera's lens, meaning the image is being digitized backward.

You can either flip all the slides in the trays (very time consuming) or simply flip them all in software once they have been digitized.

While the time necessary to set up the equipment and modify the projector may seem like a lot, once everything is set up, the actual digitization process is quicker. Some patrons may be reluctant to learn the process, but with a little patience and foresight, it can be the right method for some patrons, saving them lots of time.

THE VIDEO DIGITIZATION PROCESS

Things get a bit more complicated with video. Even with advances in the power of your average computer today, video in the digital realm is still relatively resource intensive.

This is not to dissuade you from digitizing your video, rather to give you some perspective on the time and resource requirements associated with it. Photos and documents are convenient because they are static, small entities of information. Video is linear and varied, and ultimately results in much more data. Essentially, video is just a sequence of moving photos, and it may help to think of it like that to gain some appreciation for what is actually happening when you digitize video.

While scanning 10,000 photos is a large project, a five-minute video is about the same thing. On average, a video displays 30 frames (or photos) per second. A five-minute video results in 9000 frames. This is a lot of data.

The digitization happens in real time, meaning your hour-long home videos will take an hour to digitize. There are a few caveats here. Some of the equipment digitizes your video straight to DVD. This is convenient and easy, but limits your video to the DVD. Other than a few minutes of setup and 5–10 minutes for finalizing your disc, the process takes about as long as the original video is itself.

When you digitize video to the computer, it has to ultimately save it to a specific format, such as MOV, MP4, or AVI. These all require reprocessing the video, or in other words, converting each of those thousands of frames to another format. This can take some time, depending on the length of the video and the power of your computer.

Anatomy of a Video File

Video formats can be a bit tough to wrap your head around, especially with different terms being thrown around interchangeably. Just like PPI and DPI are often used in place of one another, the same goes for *formats* and *codecs,* two terms used to describe the type of video file.

Formats and codecs refer to the different file types you can save your video as. This is important to understand for a few reasons. First is file size. Video files are large, usually measured in GB, and each format has different settings.

You can usually change things like the resolution (size of the video) and the bitrate (compression settings) for both the video and the audio. These all have an effect on the size of the file and the quality of the video itself.

The format you choose also depends on where you would like to play the video back. Luckily, with some free software at the least, you can play practically any video format on any computer. Some TVs support a handful of specific formats, and mobile devices usually support a specific list of formats as well.

File Format

Video files have two parts: the container and the codec. Together, these two parts form the file format. An example would be a Quicktime video file (the container) encoded with the h.264 codec. In everyday language, someone might refer to it as a Quicktime file.

Container

A container is what we generally think of as the file type. It is the code that tells the video playback software how to display and run the video.

Common containers include Quicktime, AVI, MPEG, MPEG4, and Flash.

Codec

The codec, which is short for compressor/decompressor, is the device that stores (compresses) and plays (decompresses) the file. Video files are very resource intensive. They are essentially thousands or millions of photo files playing in sequence, so in order to keep the file size manageable, they are compressed for storage and transmission, only to be decompressed in real time for display (Case, 2015).

Common codecs include H.264 (MPEG-4), H.262 (MPEG-2), and Windows Media (WMV).

Bitrate

The bitrate is the size of the video file per second of data. You will usually see this expressed as kilobits, or megabits per second (KBPS, MBPS). Typically, the higher the bit rate, the higher the quality of the video, since it is including more information per frame of video (Ozer, 2009).

Transcoding

Transcoding, or converting, is the act of changing a video from one format to another. This includes changing both the container and the codec, or one and not the other. People may also refer to this as converting, rendering or encoding.

Frame Rate

Videos, or what were once called motion pictures, are just that, pictures in motion. They are a series of still images, played in sequence, at a quick enough rate to form the illusion of motion.

Frame rate (or FPS for frames per second) is how many frames (images) are displayed per second.

Classic cinema was shot at 24FPS, or the least amount of frames necessary to provide the illusion of motion without any detectable flicker, or space between frames. Most modern video is shot or recorded at 30FPS or higher. Some video is still produced at 24FPS to simulate the classic film look.

Resolution

Just like digital photos, digital video has resolution as well, which is a measure of the size and quality of the frame. Standard definition, or SD video, which is what basic television was for decades, is measured as 640 × 480 pixels.

Now, high definition, or HD, footage is the norm. There are two resolutions that qualify as HD. These are 720, or 1440 × 720 pixels, and 1080, which is 1920 × 1080 pixels.

We have even begun to see 2K, 4K, and 8K video. While these are extremely high-quality resolutions, they have not made their way into everyday digitization projects at this point. They are 2000, 4000 and 8000 pixel wide videos, respectively.

Progressive and Interlaced

You will always see 720 HD video labeled as 720p, and 1080 HD video labeled as either 1080p or 1080i. The *p* stands for progressive, which means that the series of lines that are drawn on a screen (from top to bottom) are displayed sequentially. The *i* stands for interlaced, meaning that the screen displays odd numbered lines first, and even lines second.

Progressive is regarded as high quality, so you could argue that while a 720p video is of a lower resolution, its image may be of a higher quality than a 1080i video.

Aspect Ratio

A video's aspect ratio is the proportional relationship between its height and width. For the purpose of digitization, you will likely encounter the two most common aspect ratios, which are 4:3 and 16:9.

4:3 is the traditional ratio prevalent in TV and computer monitors for decades. When digitizing analog formats, they are most likely in a 4:3 ratio. 16:9, or widescreen, has become much more prevalent as the standard aspect ratio for HD video and digital television.

You will want to keep the aspect ratio when digitizing. For example, digitizing a 4:3 video to 16:9 will result in letter boxing, or black bars on the left and right sides of the video so that 4:3 image will fit within the 16:9 field. There is no advantage to this, only wasted file size. If you force a 4:3 video in 16:9, or vice versa, the image will just distort and stretch.

NTSC and PAL

NTSC and PAL are different standards used for broadcasting video over television infrastructure. NTSC is used mostly in North America and PAL in much of Europe.

The main takeaway here is not the technical difference, but that some VHS tapes that were formatted for PAL will play only in VHS players made for the European market. There are VHS players that will play both formats, which may be necessary if you work with a patron who has a PAL tape. PAL resolutions are also often a bit different than their NTSC counterparts.

Previewing Your Video

One of the challenges in digitization is organizing your assets and understanding what you are working with. Rather than diving right in, it is a good idea to look through your materials first. This is especially helpful if you have a large collection of tapes to digitize.

Previewing your movies allows you to curate, or edit on the fly the parts you would like to include. Chances are that not all of your movies are gold, or maybe there are segments you would prefer to leave out if you are giving copies to a local history collection.

This step is important! Not only for video, but also for other materials. Digitization takes time, space, and tools. Make sure you have properly gone through your collection of materials and are digitizing media that matters. If it is not important or worth digitizing, it may not be worth storing or spending the time on it.

Choosing a File Format and Settings

Choosing a file format depends largely on the final destination, as well as the original source. Do you want to store the file on a DVD? Is this something you would like to share on YouTube? What resolution should a VHS tape be? These outcomes will determine the file format you will want to choose.

Next, you will find some guidelines that will give you an idea of what format, codec, and other settings you might want for specific situations.

First, it is important to know the quality of your source. For example, HD video offers greater quality than VHS tapes. Therefore, it does not make much sense to digitize a VHS tape to an HD format. You will simply be making a file that is larger than it needs to be, without gaining any quality. Remember, garbage in, garbage out. You cannot make source material better simply by converting it to a higher-quality format. The quality must be there to begin with.

It is worth clarifying that you can sometimes improve upon the source at a later time. While converting a VHS tape to HD video will not make it look any better, there are software and other tools that can help you do things like enhance the color of the video, clean-up audio, and edit different segments together.

There are all sorts of variations and other rare formats, but this list covers common formats. The resolutions listed next are approximations. Many competing formats had resolutions that were similar, but not always exact to one another.

While resolution is not the only factor, it is a main component that determines the size of the video. Some formats have better audio quality than others, while others offered negligible increases in resolution.

VHS, VHS-C, Video8, and Betamax

≈480×320

Hi8 and Super VHS

≈530×480

DVD, Digital8, and MiniDV

≈720 × 480

Blu-Ray and HD Video Files

≈1280 × 720, 1920 × 1080

By knowing the resolution of your source file, you can digitize them into a digital video with the same resolution, giving you the appropriate file size without any unnecessary changes to the resulting file.

When exporting a video file, you can play around with various formats, bitrates, resolutions, and other settings to see how it will affect size. Most software gives you an estimated file size before committing to the process.

File Size

File size plays a role in which storage methods are feasible, the money you will need to invest in storage, and how long it will take for files to upload or transfer.

The length, file format, resolution, and compression settings all play a role in the final size of any given video file. This means that the size of a file cannot be predicted in exact terms, but many common formats and resolutions can give you an estimate. The following examples may help. These are approximations, and changes in bitrate, audio quality, and other parameters will affect file size.

60 Minutes of 1080 HD Video

- Quicktime—4.9GB
- Blu-Ray H.264–30.2GB
- MPEG2 High—43.2GB
- Prores422–119GB

60 Minutes of SD Video

- Quicktime—1.2GB
- Blu-Ray H.264–4.48GB
- MPEG2 High—6.39GB
- Prores422–17.6GB

Thanks to toolstud.io for calculations on Blu-Ray, MPEG2, and Prores422 file sizes.

Physical Formats

While they may seem like a dying breed, physical formats still have their place in our world. File formats are great for the convenience and portability, but they are susceptible to the dangers and limits of digital storage.

Physical formats have the advantage of tangibility. Many people that I've worked with have decided to go with a physical format over a strictly digital format because they can hold it. It is a carryover from older generations, but being able to hold an object that represents and contains their memories is an important and human element of the process.

These formats also provide a good backup and alternative to strictly digital storage. While they are prone to wear and tear, they are insurance against failures like a sudden hard drive crash or corrupt file.

DVD

While still considered an SD format, DVD did offer a sizable increase in resolution over VHS tapes and other analog formats, and had the added convenience of being digital. This meant exact copies, enhanced features, and better quality, including better audio.

Blu-Ray

Blu-Ray is the format for HD video on physical media that won the market and is most widely available now. It provides a sizable increase in resolution of DVD, and is at HD levels, with increased quality in both video, audio, and has other enhanced features.

THE MOTION PICTURE DIGITIZATION PROCESS

Reel-to-reel film is a whole other beast when it comes to digitization. Due to the age and brittleness of film and the varying reliability of projectors, this can be quite a challenge.

If the film is in good condition, it often suffers at the hands of an old projector. The feeding mechanism may not work correctly, or the sprocket wheel that guides the film may be misaligned and can tear into the film.

However, if you are able to work with film in good condition and a working projector, there are DIY methods. You can project the film into a telecine box, and record the reflection with an HD camera a digital camera.

I will say upfront that if you are looking for the best quality, you will need to bring your film to a professional service, such as legacybox.com, that has the proper equipment for digitizing your film in the best way, or look into funding for the professional equipment outlined in Chapter 4.

Many of the professional services have devices called a telecine, which, rather than recording an image of the moving film, pulls the film through, with a sprocketless drive (much less prone to damaging the film), and scans each frame as an individual image. These images are then compiled into a video file, resulting in the best quality possible.

Off-the-Wall Method

This method results in mediocre quality, and is recommended as a quick method to make a digital copy for the purposes of identifying the content of the film, or just an access copy.

Essentially, you project the film onto a wall or screen, preferably a surface with as little texture and character as possible. You then use a digital camera, such as a camcorder or DSLR, to record video of the projected image. It will need to be slightly off angle since the camera will have to be either above, below, or on either side of the projector. Because of this slight angle difference, the film will not project as a perfect rectangle, but for access copies, it is an acceptable flaw. Depending on the quality of the surface, film, lens and bulb, results may vary.

This method is also prone to flickering. This has to do with a difference in frame rates between the projector and digital cameras. Most film was shot at 18 frames per second, while video is usually shot at 24–30 frames per second. Due to this difference, for every x number of frames, the camera and projector will be out of sync and drop a frame.

The best solution to this problem is to use a projector with adjustable speed. In that case, you can speed up or slow down the film until the flicker is reduced. Results will not be perfect, but the flicker can be minimized.

However, the film will now be recorded at an unnatural speed. At this point, you can bring the digital video file into an editing program like iMovie or Final Cut and adjust the speed of the video until it looks right.

Modified Projector

If you are not afraid to get your hands a little dirty, you can look into modifying your projector so that the film's image projects directly into the camera. The benefit of this is that the image passes through few lenses and surfaces, resulting in a truer image.

There is no standard way to go about this, but the general idea is to prop your camera directly in front of the projector and align it so that the image projects straight into the camera's sensor. There would be no lens on the camera.

You will need to rig up a way to attach the camera to the projector so that they do not move while recording. Obviously, this method requires some ingenuity and a fair amount of research into your exact projector and camera, but it can be done, and results can be very good.

This is like the carousel scanner method put forth in the scanning section, but with a film projector. It also requires modifying the projector, specifically the light, the lens, and recording the video with a DSLR camera.

This video (https://vimeo.com/20950590) provides insight into how one man went about this with very good results.

Telecine Adapter

Telecines were popular in the 1980s when many people were transferring their films to VHS tapes for easy viewing. These are essentially boxes with a mirror inside, and a mount for the camera.

You begin by projecting your film into the telecine, and mounting your digital camera on the other end with a view window. There is a mirror inside, placed at an angle, so that the camera can record an image off the mirror. Again, depending on the quality of the film, projector, and condition of the telecine, results will vary.

These units can be found used on places like eBay. For example, you could search for the Sony VCR-4, or the Quasar Film-Tape Converter.

Film Scanners

Film scanners give you the best quality results, but usually with very expensive equipment and a longer timeline. Rather than using a digital camera to shoot video of a moving image, projected onto a wall, mirror or into the camera itself, a film scanner works frame by frame. Each image on the reel is scanned as an image file, maybe a JPEG or TIFF, and is then compiled into a video file.

This gives you much greater quality and allows for correction of each frame. The best film scanners are sprocketless. Rather than using sprocket wheels to move the film through the scanner, which runs the risk of damaging old warped film, it uses rollers to gently move the film through. This is a safer method, and results in a very high-quality file.

The RetroScan, mentioned in the previous chapter, is probably the most accessible way to use a telecine for digitizing film.

THE AUDIO DIGITIZATION PROCESS

With photos, documents, and videos, we have been relying on our eyes for digitization. Now, we turn to our ears. However, just like photos and video, audio deals with many of the same things, such as different formats, quality, compression, and other options.

Sample Rate

In digital audio, the sound is built up of parts called samples. The sample rate is how many samples of audio are played per second. As with many other measurements, the higher this number, the great the quality of the audio.

For example, CD quality audio is encoded at 44,100 samples per second, or 44.1 KHz. In comparison, cassette tapes are usually around 14–18 KHz, and telephones at 3.6 KHz.

Unless you get into more serious audio production 44.1 KHz is a good standard when digitizing audio. There are other factors, such as format and compression settings that affect the sound quality as well, but for our purposes, this is about as far as we need to go with sample rate.

Formats

Audio has compressed and uncompressed formats as well. Some of these you may have worked with before, such as MP3 files.

WAV and AIFF

While technically different, I have grouped these together since they are almost identical. WAV files are the standard uncompressed audio formats for Windows, and AIFF files the standard for Macs. However, they will both play natively on either platform, have nearly identical file sizes, and serve the same purpose.

Just like TIFF files for photos, WAV and AIFF files have large file sizes, but retain full quality because they are uncompressed. You are probably familiar with this quality, since this is the format that audio CDs are based off of, often referred to as CD quality.

The one advantage that AIFF has over WAV is its support for metadata, like album cover art, artist, lyrics, which may prove useful within the wider context of a digitization project.

FLAC

FLAC is a format that is not as common or popular as MP3 and WAV/AIFF, but offers the benefits of both. FLAC is considered a lossless, but compressed format. Because it is lossless, there is no loss in audio quality, yet is able to compress the file into a smaller file size. The result is like a ZIP file, but for audio.

MP3

Chances are that you are familiar with and have even used MP3 files before. We cannot forget that this format was responsible for a revolution in music and audio, starting back in the late 1990s, with the advent of Napster and pocket-sized MP3 players.

Why did this format have such a big impact? Just like with JPEGs, MP3 files are very compressed, but retain enough quality to be enjoyed and listened to. Until MP3s came around, a whole collection of music took up a large amount of physical space with CDs, cassettes, or records. The same was true digitally, since uncompressed files like AIFF and WAVs took up enormous amounts of storage space. This was especially true 15 years ago when the average user's hard drive was much smaller. You would have no space left on your computer after digitizing as many as 9 or 10 albums.

With MP3s, you could fit 7 to 10 times more material. This allowed people to fit large collections of music on a much smaller amount of digital storage. This led to the prevalence of MP3 players and the iPod.

This difference does come at a cost, and that is compression. Just as JPEGs discard information in an image in the name of a smaller file size, MP3s discard of certain frequencies to achieve a more manageable size. MP3s will remove certain high-end and low-end frequencies, least likely to be detected by the listener. However, there is often a detectable loss in sound quality.

You can choose the level of compression on any given MP3, and achieve a balance of the correct file size, and a quality that you deem listenable or acceptable.

AAC

Similar to MP3s, but with higher-sound quality, are AAC files. It is promoted heavily by Apple and plays in all their devices. It is also lossy, but sounds better than comparable MP3s, especially at lower bitrates. It can have many extensions, such as M4A and MP4.

Reel-to-Reel Audio

Just as reel-to-reel film poses challenges in digitizing, the same goes for audio. The condition and size of your tape all play a big role in the feasibility of preserving your audio, as does the player you have.

There are no readily available reel-to-reel audio players on the market, but there are plenty of used machines on eBay. If you have the knowledge required to run one of these machines (calibration, maintenance), you can likely connect its outputs to your digitization interface. From there it is like recording from any other device.

Mono and Stereo

Mono audio is a single channel, whereas stereo is dual channel audio, or left and right. All digital audio formats can be set as either mono or stereo, and it should be dependent on the source material.

Oftentimes, radio or voice-centric recordings will be in mono, and music will be in stereo. This is not always the case, so you will want to check with your source audio.

Bitrate

Just like with video, the bitrate for audio is the amount of data included per unit of time. The higher the bitrate, the better quality the audio file.

Specifically, bitrate is something you can choose with MP3s. They typically range from as low as 32KBPS, up to 320KBPS. Anything under 128KBPS will have a noticeable loss in audio quality, but above that, the average listener loses its ability to tell the difference.

For many, the difference between a high quality, 320KBPS stereo MP3 file and a CD quality AIFF file is indistinguishable, yet the MP3 has a much smaller file size.

Choosing a File Format and Settings

Again, it is important to know the final application of your digitized audio. Knowing your end goal will help you choose the correct format and settings best suited for your recording.

Keep in mind that while you can always make a copy in various formats, doing so does not always make sense. When you have a high-quality, large file-size format, like WAV or AIFF, and you need something smaller for easier distribution online, converting it to MP3 makes sense. You are achieving a smaller file size, and losing some audio quality, for the sake of convenience and speed. This is a common thing to do with audio.

However, if you start with an MP3, but would like a higher-quality version, converting it to a WAV or AIFF will give you only a larger file size, not better quality. When starting with an MP3, you are beginning with low quality. You cannot gain that back by simply converting to a format that allows for higher fidelity. If you need that quality, you will have to get the original source for the recording, then digitize it at a high quality.

This is why it usually makes sense to digitize at high quality, then make copies in other formats for ease of distribution and speed.

Previewing Your Audio

Just as with video, it is a good idea to preview your audio before you commit to recording it. You have two choices here. You can find a cassette deck, turntable, or other device to play back your audio. Go ahead and listen through, and take note of the times you would like to record. This way, you are prepared to record only the parts you need.

The second way is to connect your recording device to the computer. There are turntables and cassette decks that have USB connections, which make them very easy to set up. Or, if you have the Canopus video digitization interface mentioned earlier in the book, you can connect a normal cassette deck or turntable through that. Once the device is connected and you have pulled up the appropriate software, you can begin to listen back to your audio. With everything set up to go, you are ready to click record when the correct material comes on.

Whether you are using Garageband, Audacity, or some other audio program, setting up your connections is a pretty standard process. The device you have connected to the computer needs to be set as an input. This tells the computer to record sound from that specific device. So, in your program, you would set the input to your specific device. As for the output, that does not need to change. That can be the standard output or speakers for your computer.

Many of these devices will have a recording level or input gain knob on them. This lets you set the volume at which your audio records at. You want to make sure that the loudest parts of the audio can pass through without distorting, while the quiet parts are recorded at a loud enough, listenable volume.

THE RESTORATION PROCESS

One of the best parts about digitization is the ability to enhance, fix, or correct any flaws. While there is a definite charm to our materials the way they are, being able to correct is a definite advantage.

This ability can be especially useful when you choose a handful of important documents to display in your home or present them for some other use.

With the software available to us today, there are very few things that are not possible. Keep in mind that enhancements and corrections require a fair amount of learning, no matter what software you choose. Basic corrections like adjusting color contrast and exposure can be done with a few hours of learning.

You probably recognize the title Photoshop, which is synonymous today with image editing and performing miracles on damaged or flawed photos. More in-depth corrections such as replacing a torn part of the photo, putting color into a black-and-white photo, or editing together a video with voiceovers, music, titles and more can be done, but only with proper training.

This is just to set proper expectations. As with anything else, you will be able to find great satisfaction and in learning the more in-depth corrections and enhancements to your photos, video, or audio.

Photos and Documents

You do not want to risk damaging the original any further by attempting to repair it. However, using software, you can do your best to fix the digitized version.

Some scanning software, such as Epson Scan, comes with features to address these problems. Epson Scan has a dust removal feature that detects dust while scanning, and removes it from the image. It also has a feature that removes scratches from film and slides. Both features have different levels of intensity; however, their effectiveness differs based on the context of the image.

The biggest name in photographic correction, restoration, and editing is Adobe Photoshop. It is so widely known; it is often used as a verb—for example, "That image was obviously Photoshopped."

Photoshop is a broad program, offering the ability not only to edit and manipulate photos, but also to create works of art from nothing, work with 3D models, and even edit video.

There is also a free app called GIMP. It offers many of the capabilities that Photoshop does, but is not as polished, or in certain cases, not as powerful.

For Mac specifically, there is Pixelmator, a newcomer in recent years that rivals Photoshop in some ways, and is an indie favorite among Mac users.

Most of these programs offer tools for specifically fixing scratches, blemishes, tears, color casts, and missing pieces.

Video

Much like photos, videos come with a wide range of flaws that may need to be addressed after digitization. Many home videos were taken on affordable, yet lower-quality equipment available to the average consumer. These videos often have poor exposure and color, both of which can be adjusted after the fact.

One of the most widely used programs for editing video in library digital media labs is iMovie. While it has its own quirks, iMovie offers users a way to edit their video, adjust things like color, contrast, and exposure, and add music and photos as well.

Other programs, like Premiere Pro and Final Cut offer much deeper and advanced capabilities for not only correcting, but also editing video.

Audio

Older audio formats were prone to many noise issues. Tape is well known for its hiss, and records are known for cracks and pops. Luckily, there is software available that can help us remove or reduce some of those flaws.

Restoration is not always necessary though. Some of these "flaws" are what give the audio its charm and character from another time. Fixing these issues is your decision.

There are many apps that will aid you in cleaning up and restoring audio. A few of them are outlined next. This list is in no way exhaustive, but offers a range of programs that are free and paid for.

Audacity

Audacity offers a generic noise removal tool. It allows you to capture a noise profile, and then from that, it will apply the reduction to the rest of the sound.

Using that profile, you then apply the removal to the rest of the recording, and can choose the level of removal parameters, like the reduction amount in decibels (dB), sensitivity, and frequency smoothing.

Garageband

Garageband offers even less granularity with the settings of noise removal, but offers some nonetheless.

In a track's Smart Controls window, there is an option to enable a noise gate. A noise gate will only let sound play if it is above a certain volume threshold. By adjusting the threshold slider and listening, you can find the sweet spot between blocking out the background hiss, and allowing the desire sound through.

The biggest drawback to a noise gate is that the noise is still active while the desired sound is playing, but is removed in between sections you want to hear.

Adobe Audition

Adobe Audition is a favorite among broadcast professionals. Unlike Garageband and other popular audio production suites, like Pro Tools and Logic Pro, Audition is aimed at editing audio, not specifically music or multitrack productions. It has great tools for editing noise, hiss, scratches pops, and other unwanted elements, as well as editing parts together.

Izotope RX

Izotope RX is a professional level tool for cleaning up audio. In fact, that is its focus. The other programs outlined are multipurpose tools, meant for recording and mixing audio, but they do offer some tools for restoring your sound.

Izotope has the best restoration tools because that is its specialty. It offers the ability to remove crackle, pop, hiss, hum, and other noise. It generally works by having the user capture a sound profile, analyzing it, then removing that analyzed sound from the rest of the recording.

Chapter 6

Storage and Backups

So far, our focus has been on digitization, but that is only the first part. Once our materials are digitized, it is time to store and backup our collection.

Storage entails more than just letting your files sit around on a hard drive somewhere. We want to be intentional in where we store our files, how we name and organize them, and in making copies and backups. This section will outline all details relevant to storing your collection.

Hopefully, the impression you have gotten by now is that no form of storage is perfect. The physical, original documents are susceptible to wear and tear, as well as other environmental factors, and the digital copies are prone to hard drive crashes, accidental deletions, and other issues.

It is best if you make a habit of regularly backing up your digital copies in multiple places and in different forms so your data is as safe as it can be.

Storage and backup are core tenets of good digitization practice. Just like digitizing itself provides a backup of your files, storing and backing up do the same thing. Having multiple, redundant copies in different places only ensures that your data is safe.

Let us clarify exactly what is meant by storage, backups, and archives.

STORAGE

In general, storage is where your data is sitting at the moment. For most people, that is the primary hard drive on their computer. It is easily accessible, recent, and relevant. In this sense, storage is where your digitized files sit right out of the gate.

The problem with storage is that it is your only copy. It is not safe from the issues that plague digital files. They may be accidentally deleted, lost, or misplaced.

Think of storage as a sort of purgatory. It is where files sit while the real plan for safety and backup is devised. What we need most are backups.

BACKUPS

Backups are essential to any data management strategy. This is where your data becomes much safer and more reliable. A backup is simply a copy of your current files in a different place. This can be an external hard drive, a flash drive, DVD, or some sort of cloud service. A good backup strategy includes a regular and frequent schedule in multiple locations. This ensures current data and safety.

ARCHIVES

Archives refer to long-term, permanent storage. These are files you are certain of keeping, but do not need immediate access to. For the sake of this book, archives and backups are often interchangeable. At a professional level, they are certainly different, but for your average person, backups often act as long-term storage, depending on the medium they are stored to.

FILE SAVING

One key decision in setting up your digitization service is to decide how file handling and storage should be done. How will patrons store their files? Do they need to bring their own storage device? How do you ensure privacy and security on the computer from patron to patron? These are all decisions you will want to make ahead of time.

Most libraries require patrons to save files to their own storage device, since it provides greater security and privacy, and relieves the library of the responsibility of dealing with the potentially large amount of files and storage required to house everyone's digitized materials. Family items can often be personal, so being able to ensure that no one will see the digitized material's once the patron is done with their session is important. It is also good customer service to provide a clean slate for the next patron to use the space.

Deep Freeze is a popular piece of software that many labs use to make sure that each patron starts with a clean slate. It allows you to set up the computer in a particular default state, or the state the computer should be in whenever someone new begins their digitization session. This would likely include all the required software and drivers for your digitization equipment, as well as default settings you would like in place. For example, in a lab where most patrons are scanning 35mm negatives at 2400 DPI, it would not hurt to make that the default setting in the scanning software to make things a bit easier and quicker for a large portion of your user base.

Every time the computer is restarted, a patron's files are deleted, and the computer is restored to its default state. You will want to make restarting the computer a habit for patrons finishing up their sessions, as well as having staff restart the computer between users. Because of this finality, it is crucial that patrons understand this. They will need to make sure that they have saved their progress to their storage device.

To make things easy for the patrons, let them know what storage devices work best. Usually a flash drive or external hard drive are easiest, or they can use cloud storage, such as Google Drive and Dropbox, if they are familiar and have enough space on their accounts. You may also want to have some of your own storage devices on hand for checkout, in case a patron forgets their own, or there is an issue with the storage they have supplied.

Because digitization projects can involve massive files, specifically video, you will want to offer large amounts of storage and the fastest transfer speeds possible. At this point, USB 3.0 is the most widely used high-speed transfer format. Make sure to purchase flash drives and external hard drives that support USB 3.0. Your computer must also support it as well to take advantage of the speed, otherwise it will downscale to USB 2.0 speeds. For example, if a patron spends two hours digitizing VHS tapes, and now has 30GB video file, that may take another 60 minutes to transfer via USB 2.0. I have often run into a situation like this, and can put an unexpected time burden on the user, or interrupt the scheduled reservations for the lab. By offering faster speeds, you can reduce the friction of the process and get patrons in and out as scheduled.

Drive formats are something else worth considering. Each drive you use is structured with a specific format. For Windows, it is often NTFS; for Mac, it is HFS+ (also known as Mac OS Journaled); and flash drives often use FAT32 and ExFat. ExFat is a good format to have your drive formatted since it works on both Windows and Mac platforms. FAT32 works as well, but has a 4GB file size limit, meaning it will not be that useful for video digitization since those files often run well over 4GB. We will dive deeper into formats at the end of this chapter.

Be careful before formatting any drives, since all data will be lost. If a customer needs to format his or her drive, make sure he or she understands. The patron can always copy his or her drive's content to the computer first, format the drive, copy it back if need be.

It is also worth noting that while most digitization projects' files are straightforward, anyone using iMovie for a project may run into a bit of confusion. While most software titles simply output a file with the digitized result, like a JPEG or WAV file, iMovie has a project file, and a final exported movie file.

The iMovie library is what iMovie uses to assemble a project. You can think of it like a roadmap that tells iMovie—for example, to use these few segments of these specific movie clips, this handful of photos, and this background music. Once the movie is assembled the way the user likes it, he or she can *share,* or export the movie to a single file for people to view. If someone is in the midst of an iMovie project and wants to save it to work on later, he or she will have to move the entire iMovie library to an external drive.

iMovie will work only with HFS+ (Mac OS Journaled) drives, so make sure you have one plugged into your Mac. You will then go to *File > Library > Open Library*. This will let you create a new iMovie library on your flash drive or external hard drive. You will now see two iMovie projects displayed in your left side navigation in iMovie. You can now simply drag the project from the main drive to your external drive, and it will copy over the project and all assets.

3–2–1 RULE

This rule is a great guideline for keeping your data safe. It calls for three copies of your data, in two different formats, with one of them stored off-site. If you can remember this rule, your data will be much safer.

WHERE TO STORE

We know that storage and backup is important, but how do we go about this? Let us find out.

Primary Hard Drive

Copies on your computer's primary hard drive are not technically a backup, but a local copy, ideally for quick access. Since your computer is used everyday, its hard drive receives a lot of use and is more susceptible to issues than a drive meant only for backup.

While it is nice to have your assets within reach, do not leave the only copy of your files on your primary hard drive. You are going to want copies elsewhere. On a Windows machine, this is your C: Drive, and on a Mac, it is usually labeled *Macintosh HD* by default.

If you are familiar with building or modifying a computer, you can install a second hard drive. This option gives you the advantage of having your important data on a secondary drive, that is not as frequently accessed, but quick to reach, and likely large in capacity.

Internal hard drives are very affordable as well. You can easily find a 1TB drive for around $50, and up to 3TB for under $100.

External Hard Drive

Your next line of defense is an external hard drive. These are easy to find, affordable, offer plenty of storage space, and easy to work with.

These drives usually have a USB connection, which is widely universal. If you need a different connection, say FireWire, eSATA, or Thunderbolt, there are options for those as well, though they may be harder to find and are more expensive. A USB 3.0 connection is preferable since it has fast transfer speeds, which is great for larger collections of data.

Another benefit of an external hard drive over internal is that it is portable, and can be accessed from any computer. They will also help out with the 3–2–1 rule, giving you the option of easily storing off-site.

Flash Drive

Flash drives are like external hard drives, although they are much smaller in stature, typically hold less storage, and do not transfer files as quickly. They are more affordable and more convenient.

If your assets do not amount to much, a few inexpensive flash drives may be a quick and easy answer. You may have received a flash drive for free as a promotional item at a conference, or you may have bought one specifically for storage. Free flash drives typically hold anywhere from 2GB-8GB of storage. Higher end drives transfer at higher speeds and may have sizes of 64GB or larger.

Because they are more affordable, they are great for making many copies of your data, and storing multiple copies off-site or in different locations.

DVDs and CDs

DVDs and CDs are another option for storing your files. They provide great portability, and are easily copied and reproduced. They do, however, have smaller storage capacities. CDs typically top out at around 700MB, and DVDs, at 4.7GB.

You will probably have to split your data across several discs. This can be inconvenient since burning a disc takes some time, and moving data between CDs and DVDs and other discs is more cumbersome than using flash drives and hard drives.

The Cloud

This entails both cloud storage and cloud backups. These are files placed on Internet connected storage, or servers. This ensures access from any device with an Internet connection, as well as the technical support of whichever service you choose.

BACKUPS

Let us take a look at the various types of backups.

Redundant Backups

Redundant storage entails copying and storing your collection in multiple places, using multiple methods. This ensures that your collection is safe, even if one or more of your other copies is compromised.

Although most information is now digital, new storage methods are fool-proof. They all have their advantages and drawbacks. While digital storage is not susceptible to the same problems that analog materials are, hard drives fail, cloud storage is hacked, and flash drives are lost.

Backblaze, a cloud backup and storage service provider, performed a now somewhat famous study of 40,000 of its hard drives used to store its customers' data. They found that a drive will encounter three failure phases. Phase one, which is 1.5 years long, shows that 5.1 percent of hard drives fail. Phase two, the next 1.5 years, dips to a failure rate of 1.4 percent. Finally, phase three, the next year, jumps to an 11.8 percent failure rate. About 50 percent of hard drives will make it to their sixth year. What does this tell us? Digital storage is imperfect, and backups are a must! (Sebastian, 2013).

Hitachi looks to be the most reliable, even across different storage sizes, with Western Digital next, and Seagate in last, with survival rates varying widely by storage size, but higher overall.

Keep in mind, these drives are always on, being used to store customer's data. Regardless, it gives you a sense of a typical hard drive's lifespan. More importantly, it shows you that while digital storage has many advantages, it is still prone to failure, and overall, a shorter lifespan than earlier analog media.

This is not to dissuade you from using hard drives, just to give you a real-istic perspective on their lifespan and behaviors. As with any technology, you will hear horror stories about any brand. As long as you are diligent about multiple backups, you should be in good hands.

Physical Locations

Now that you have three different backups, it is a good idea to make sure they are in physically different locations. Copied all your data to three hard drives? It does not do you much good to leave them all under the same roof. If something happens to your home, your digitized assets are gone too.

An ideal setup would look something like this:

- Files stored locally on an external hard drive, in the residence for quick and convenient access.
- Files stored on an external hard drive, off-site, maybe at a relative's house, or in a safety deposit box.
- Files stored in the cloud, on a service such as Google Drive, Dropbox, or iCloud.

Cloud Storage and Backups

With your local backups taken care of, you will now want to take a look into backing up your data to the cloud.

There are two different types of cloud solutions. There is cloud storage, and cloud backup. They are essentially the same thing, but the way in which you interface with them is different.

With cloud storage, you have the freedom to upload, download, and drag and drop files as you would locally on your computer. It has the flexibility and convenience of the file system on your machine.

Cloud backup, on the other hand, is more of an entire backup solution for your computer. It is meant to backup your entire machine, or specific files or hard drives, in the background while you work or are away from your computer.

As with the other methods mentioned, the cloud has its own advantages and disadvantages. The cloud takes the responsibility of technical issues off the user's shoulders. This allows you to simply organize and access your files, without having to be bothered by any technical concerns. It also allows you the convenience of accessing your data from anywhere there is an Internet connection.

On the other hand, while you do not have to concern yourself with that technical side of the cloud, you leave the fate of your data to the service you choose. Cloud storage is also vulnerable to data breaches, technical failures, and human error, such as when Flickr (a photo sharing website) accidentally deleted a photo blogger's account that held over 4,000 photos (Cloud Storage, 2011).

The cloud also poses a convenient and often affordable option for backing up your files. It also has the advantage of being supported by technology professionals, redundantly backed up within the cloud service, and accessible from anywhere with an Internet connection.

Many people have cloud accounts whether they know it or not. Have an Apple product? Chances are you have an Apple ID, which means you have an iCloud account with 5GB of storage. The same goes for Google. A Google or Gmail account leaves with you 15GB of online cloud storage. An account with Microsoft gives you 5GB of space through its service OneDrive. And these are all free, so these may be a good place to start.

However, your digitized collection may be much larger than those free tiers of service. In that case, many of them offer larger storage capacities for a monthly or yearly fee.

Another thing to keep in mind with a cloud service is that placing large amounts of data into the cloud will take awhile to backup. Throwing a few photos onto a cloud service will only take a few seconds, a minute at the most with a modern broadband connection, to upload. However, a collection of 30GB of materials may take a day or so to upload, depending on your collection.

Cloud Storage

Here is a rundown of some popular cloud services that many people use for storage.

iCloud

iCloud is Apple's cloud solution for syncing data and backing up files. For most, iCloud syncs data like contacts, calendars, and photos across their Apple devices. With the latest update to iCloud, they have added iCloud Drive, which allows a user to manually manage files and folders, which is ideal for placing files into the cloud for easy access.

By default, a user receives 5GB of space, although some of this is taken up by other data, such as iPhone or iPad backups, contacts, music, or other items.

You will likely want to add more space. Apple offers the following upgraded storage options:

* 50GB for $0.99 per month
* 200GB for $2.99 per month
* 1TB for $9.99 per month

Google Drive

When you create a Google account, you get access to all sorts of Google Apps, such as Gmail, Calendar, and Drive. Google Drive is where you can store files in the cloud. By simply signing up for an account, Google Drive gives you 15GB of storage. This includes your e-mail as well. The following upgrade options are available.

* 100GB for $1.99 per month
* 1TB for $9.99 per month
* 10TB for $99.99 per month
* 20TB for $199.99 per month
* 30TB for $299.99 per month

OneDrive

OneDrive is Microsoft's cloud service. It ties in with their online office solution and outlook e-mail service. Like Google, Microsoft gives you 15GB by default.

* 50GB for $1.99 per month
* 1TB for $6.99 per month

Dropbox

Dropbox is an independent company that specializes in cloud storage. Because of this focus, they are one of the most popular cloud services. A free account gives you 2GB of storage, with the upgrade options available.

Dropbox also allows you to get more space by things like referring a friend to Dropbox, tweeting about their services, and other small tasks.

- 1TB for $9.99 per month
- Unlimited storage for $15 per user, per month (business plan)

Cloud Backup

Here is a rundown of some popular cloud services that many people use for backup. Rather than drag and drop file handling, these are meant as all-in-one backup services that protect the data on your entire computer, or in some case, connected external drives as well.

Backblaze

$50.00 per year

Carbonite

$59.99 per year

Mozy

$65.89 per year

Crashplan

$59.99 per year

Social Media as Cloud Storage

Depending on your needs, you may find another form of backup in social media, or photo, audio, and video sharing sites that allow you to share your media with others. While these are not considered true backups, it never hurts to have another copy of your media somewhere. If any of these sites prove useful for a patron, all the better, but they should never be a primary source of backup.

Sites such as Facebook and Instagram are known by the general public at this point. For most, these sites are associated with publicly sharing your photos. While this is true, and usually the intent of sites, it is not how they have to be used. Most of these services have privacy settings, where you can choose to limit sharing your content with specific users. So it is plausible to think one could limit their content to only the friends and family they would like to share with. A user can also limit their content to no one, and simply use their accounts as a place to store photos.

These backups should be considered access copies. They are convenient to access and easy to share, but most services do not allow full quality, uncompressed copies. They do not often offer the full range of organization options you would find with a file system on your computer or other photo, video, or audio specific services or apps. The common sites like, Facebook, Twitter, and Instagram simply offer an easy way to quickly access photos, albeit not in well-organized, or large collections. Their selling point is convenience and their social aspect.

That said, there are specific media sharing services, like Flickr (for photos), Vimeo (for video), and SoundCloud (for audio). Photos tend to have more options when it comes to social networks, followed by video, then audio.

Sites like Flickr (and other ones like *500px.com* and Google Photos) give you more in-depth and flexible organization options, the ability to upload full quality and uncompressed photos. These are a bit more reliable in terms of backing up. Vimeo allows similar options for video, and SoundCloud similar for audio.

The other concern here is the rights to your content. While no one wants to take the time to read the terms of service for any given website, make sure you are aware of what you are agreeing too when you sign up for any of these social media services. Terms vary for each service, but you'll want to understand what rights you may be giving up in terms of ownership, and if you're giving the service permission to use your content in a certain way.

The takeaway here is that these sites can be a nice complement to the other, more reliable methods of backing up and sharing.

World Backup Day

There is even a World Backup Day, which can be a helpful reminder to take a deeper look at your backup methods. Make sure to mark your calendars for March 31.

At *worldbackupday.com,* there are tips and tricks for getting started with backup, and even a pledge you can take and publicize to friends on Facebook and Twitter to spread the word.

They even have a street team page, where you can print out posters and flyers for your library, to spread the important word about backing up. This can be especially useful information for any sort of local history or digitization group.

RECOMMENDATIONS AND OPTIONS

There are many brands you will come across when looking into purchasing storage and backup equipment. While I will make some recommendations next, remember, redundancy is the key. Even the best equipment may fail you, so going with a recommended item does not ensure complete data safety.

External Hard Drive

There are two types of external hard drives—desktop and portable. Desktop drives are physically larger, and have a power supply that plugs in separately from the data connection to the computer. The drives themselves are larger at 3.5", compared to the 2.5" in the portable drives. Desktop drives often offer higher speeds, both in the drives themselves and in the connections offered. Portable drives are usually limited to USB connections (2.0, 3.0, and C), while desktop drives offer a number for connections such as USB, FireWire, eSATA, Thunderbolt, and others. External hard drives are also somewhat more reliable than portable drives, simply because they are typically stationary and are not as prone to accidents while being moved around.

Notable brands include Western Digital and Seagate. They tend to be the two main players in the external hard drive market. Other brands worth looking into are Iomega, LaCie.

Space gets cheaper every day, and at the time of this writing, Western Digital offers a 4TB desktop external hard drive for $129. That is a very large amount of storage for the price. To give you some perspective on size, 4TB of data can store one million songs, 300 hours of HD video, or 800,000 photos. Even 1TB would be ample space for many of your patron's digitization needs.

Flash Drive

While external hard drives are great for large amounts of data, flash drives (also known as thumb drives and jump drives), offer a more affordable, portable, and convenient solution for patrons just beginning their digitization projects.

While you do not get the same bang for your buck in terms of GB per dollar, you get a good amount of space and much convenience. Chances are, your patrons already have a flash drive or two. Most flash drives today come in sizes of at least 8GB, and range all the way up to 256GB.

One of the great things about these drives is that since they are affordable and easily portable, they are great for redundant backups. If your collection of digitized photos is 12GB, it would be easy to quickly copy those over to a few other flash drives, store them in different places, and have some redundancy in place.

There are tons of options when it comes to flash drives. Brands include SanDisk, Memorex, Lexar, Patriot and many, many more. It is difficult to make a recommendation for a specific model, since most flash drives do their job adequately. If you are really concerned about speed, you just need to make sure you are purchasing a USB 3.0 flash drive, and that the computer you are working with has USB 3.0 as well to take advantage of the speed.

DVDs and CDs

While not as convenient as external hard drives and flash drives, optical media such as DVDs and CDs offer a reliable method for archiving your digitized assets. Popping in a disc every time you want to view materials is not quite as convenient as a drive, but if properly stored, their lifespan is longer than that of hard drives and flash drives.

One of the main concerns with optical media (and ultimately, all media) is how accessible it will be. With fewer and fewer computers shipping with optical drives, it is beginning to be a challenge to access these discs. Ten years down the line, it might prove difficult for accessing these archives, much in the way that accessing a floppy disk is a challenge today.

In terms of recommendations, this is difficult as well, since like flash drives, there are so many brands and options available. Most are reliable enough, but every brand will give you some lemons every now and then. Again, this is why copies and redundancy are important. And with the affordability of optical media (it is about $20 for 50 DVDs), making copies is an easy thing to do.

Space-wise, you are looking at smaller capacities than hard drives and flash drives. CD's store about 700MB of data, and DVDs storage 4.7GB per disk.

FILENAMING CONVENTIONS

Methods for naming your files can quickly get detailed, tedious, and over-whelming. For our purposes, there are ways we can keep it simple. Since we are not working on developing huge collections for large institutions, we will not need to worry about taking some of these guidelines as far as a professional would.

However, you or your patrons may still be digitizing a large collection of materials, so there are a few things to keep in mind when naming your files to keep them in logical order, easily accessible, and properly organized.

Meaningful and Nondescriptive Names

Meaningful names contain a word that relates to the content of the materials being digitized. This makes it easy to identify the item simply by looking at the name. These words can be as generic or as descriptive as you would like. The key here is that it is something you or others will recognize quickly when skimming through the collection.

Nondescriptive titles provide no contextual insight into the files. They are usually for larger collections managed by special database software that may contain extra metadata, such as tags and other descriptors.

Name Length

Do your best to keep the file name to eight characters or fewer. This ensures backward compatibility with older operating systems and software.

Filename Extension

Some filename extensions have four or more characters, such as TIFF or JPEG. For you or your patrons' collection, keep the extension to three char-acters, JPG or TIF, for example.

Alpha-Numeric Characters

Use only alpha-numeric characters, dashes, and underscores. Other special characters may not be compatible with filename standards for various operating systems and software.

Lowercase Letters

For consistency's sake and for software compatibility, keep the entire filename lowercase.

Use Leading Zeroes

Again for consistency's sake, and for easier management, use leading zeroes. For example, if there are going to be thousands of images in your collection, the first image should be named *image-0001.jpg*, instead of *image-1.jpg*.

LIFESPAN OF ANALOG AND DIGITAL STORAGE

While digitization provides us with many benefits, such as convenience, copies, backups, and the flexibility of editing and improvements, we know at this point that it is not a perfect system. Digitization has it is limitations, and we should be wary of this when working without materials.

Hard drives are not the most reliable of storage mediums, with a failure rate of around 2–11 percent depending on the point in its lifecycle.

Flash storage, such as flash drives and new flash-based hard drives, while much faster in performance, have their own limitations as well.

For your own safety and consideration, here are the approximate lifespans of various media types, both analog and digital. Keep in mind these are approximations. There are always outliers—for example, flash drives tend to get lost long before they would break or wear out. Any media, stored properly and with great care, can last longer than predicted.

It is also important to note that with analog and digital storage, while your files, disc, or drive may be intact, there may not be a way to access those files down the road. If your photos are on a DVD, will there be DVD drives around 30 years from now to access your photos?

Analog Media

Reel-to-Reel Audio Tape

10 years of regular use. 20 years with greater care.

Cassette Tape

10 years of regular use. 20 years with greater care.

Vinyl Record

100 years of regular use.

VHS Tape

5 years of regular use. 15 years with greater care.

Super 8 Film

70 years of regular care. 100 years with greater care.

Photo Slides

50 years of regular use. 70 years with greater care.

Developed Photos

50 years of regular use. 78 years with greater care.

Digital Storage
CD

3 years of regular use. 100 years with greater care.

DVD

30 years of regular use. 100 years with greater care.

Flash Drive

10 years of regular use. 75 years with greater care.

Hard Drive

34 years of regular use. 100 years with greater care.

Solid State Drive

51 years of regular use. 100+ years with greater care.
(Jacobi, 2015)

PHYSICAL STORAGE

Whether you are finished with your digitization project and need to store your materials again, or you are just looking for more effective and secure ways to keep your memories intact, learning to properly store your items is crucial to preservation.

With such a wide variety of formats and materials, each one has its own guidelines for proper storage. Remember to do the best you can. You likely do not have the advantages that a large institution does with more advanced climate control and staff.

As mentioned previously in this book, digitization is not a total solution. It is mostly a way to make copies of your originals in a way that is affordable, convenient, and allows for editing and corrections that will not harm the original.

However, for some people, they may be digitizing so that they can free up some space and part with the originals. While it has obvious drawbacks, that is a decision for them to make.

If you have decided to get rid of the original materials, then you will not have to worry about how to keep storing them, or consider how to properly store them so that they continue on with minimal aging.

The following are some general guidelines for storing your originals so that they continue on in relatively good condition.

Many of these suggestions come from *archives.org*, which offers in-depth details into properly storing and caring for aging documentary materials. Much of this is not practical for your average citizen, so I have done my best to simplify it for practicality's sake.

Remember, do the best you can with these guidelines. You do not have to follow every rule, but you want to do a good enough job of storing and caring for these materials that they live on, hopefully for another generation or so.

It is worth mentioning that while you are going through all your materials, you might as well add an element of curation to the process. While these materials may mean a lot to you, it is important to part with pieces that do not offer any real value.

It can be overwhelming to open an old box of photos and slides, only to realize you have thousands of photos to sift through. Do you really have the time to digitize every item? Are they all even worth it?

It is important to ask yourself these questions. No one wants to admit that a photo from their precious childhood may not be good, but much of these materials were taken by average folks with no real training. That does not make these photos worth any less, but that blurry image that does not tell much of a story may not be worth digitizing, or the time it takes to clean it up, whether before scanning or afterward in Photoshop.

Take this opportunity to sift through your collection, choose the photos, letters, films, or recordings that mean the most to you, and commit to digitizing those first and foremost.

From there, you can make a second round of scans, discard items that really are not worth much to you, or resolve to keep the rest in physical form in the off chance you need to revisit the photos you deemed unworthy of digitization.

It is important to place the materials we have decided on keeping in the right conditions. There may have been mistakes made when storing these materials originally, maybe as long as 30 or 40 years ago.

Documents

Documents, including family papers, letters, bound materials, and wills should be stored in an environment with low relative humidity, between 15 percent and 65 percent, and a low, stable temperature, below 75 degrees Fahrenheit. Items should be stored in the dark, away from sunlight and air pollutants, and elevated to avoid damage from flooding, insects, or rodents.

Documents should be stored in boxes and stored flat. Ideally, each item will be placed in a polyester sleeve to further protect it from dust and other damage. Make sure to put each item in a sleeve that is larger than the document itself, to prevent edges from getting damaged. Avoid directly marking up materials with annotations or notes.

Photos

This includes photographic prints, negatives, and slides. To start, make sure to store these items at low temperatures, below 75 degrees Fahrenheit. Low temperature slows the rate of decay that can happen with all the chemicals involved in film photography and prints.

Relative humidity should be kept below 65 percent, but not too low, or below 15 percent, to prevent brittle materials. Dark, dry places make for good storage. Avoid fluctuating temperatures and humidity. Store these items in an elevated spot to avoid the potential for flood, insect, or rodent damage.

If possible, store acetate negatives, color negatives, prints, and slides at lower, cold temperatures to slow the process of deterioration. Stored at room temperature, these items can begin to fade in just a few decades.

Avoid storing any photos in such a way that corners are bent, edges are exposed or hang outside of the storage container. Find containers that are large enough for the photos to lay flat without any bending or curling. Make sure the box is the right size, so items are not moving around when transported or stored, and make sure not to place too many items in any given container. Use boxes made from materials that are lignin-free, acid-free, or buffered.

Video

Video includes any magnetic tapes or optical media from the past 40–50 years. Most commonly, these will be VHS tapes and DVDs.

Temperature and humidity are key to proper storage. Video media should be stored in an environment with stable, low temperatures, and humidity, ideally 55–70 degrees Fahrenheit, and a relative humidity of 30–55 percent.

Make sure to keep items elevated to avoid flooding damage, and exposure to insects and rodent. Avoid sunlight as well.

Placement is also important. Store tapes and discs vertically in boxes and cases. Most importantly, store tapes away from anything that produces an electromagnetic field, such as magnets or surge protectors. Avoid adhesive labels and solvent-based markers as well.

Motion Pictures

Most, if not all of the motion pictures you will encounter in a library digitization program will be 8mm, Super 8mm, or 16mm film. 16mm came out in the 1920s, 8mm in the 1930s, and Super 8mm in the 1930s, so these films will be some of the oldest materials you may encounter. As with other formats, proper storage is the key to preservation.

Ideally, these films will be stored at 55 degrees Fahrenheit with a 45 percent relative humidity. If these conditions are not practical, aim for an environment with a stable, low temperature, low humidity, and safe from sunlight and air pollutants. Keeping the film safe from water, insects, or even rodents is advised.

Places such as attics or garages, where humidity and temperature can vary wildly should be avoided. These conditions will contribute to mold growth and deterioration of the film.

Audio

Many of us have been through the carousel of new audio formats over the years. There is a good chance many patrons will have items to digitize on more than one of these formats. Following are some good storage guidelines.

Applicable to all the following formats is to store them in a low humidity, mild temperature environment, safe from the risk of flooding and pollutants.

Ideally, you want to store your audio at 55–75 degrees Fahrenheit, and in a relative humidity of 30–55 percent. Climate-controlled closets or unused rooms make for good spaces. A basement can work if it is not damp, and the items are kept elevated to prevent flooding damage or exposure to insects and rodents. Stay away from garages and attics.

All forms of audio, including vinyl, tapes (both cassettes and reels), and CDs should be stacked vertically, in their plastic cases, boxes, or sleeves. Do not stack the media directly atop one another.

Tapes especially must be stored away from electromagnetic fields, such as loudspeakers, anything with magnets, high voltage lines, and surge protectors. Data on tapes is recorded and read magnetically, so exposure to stray electromagnetic fields can destroy or corrupt the audio.

Make sure to avoid using solvent-based markers and adhesive labels. These deteriorate over time and can damage audio media.

Keep your audio away from sunlight and UBV light. This is especially important for recordable media, such as CD-Rs. On that note, recordable media is generally considered less reliable than commercially produced media. CD-Rs, specifically, use a different recording method than commercial CDs, that is less reliable over time (Archival Formats, 2015).

SERVICES AND SUPPLIES

Digitization Services

In case your library does not offer the capabilities a patron is looking for, you may want to give them a few resources for outside digitization. These may be useful for more obscure formats, or if some materials just need a professional treatment.

Legacybox.com is an online operation that makes digitization as simple as it gets. They offer a few different packages, starting at $75, for most formats you may come across. They will send you a prepaid box, which you load up and send back. Three to four weeks later, you will receive archival DVDs and dig-ital files, as well as your originals. From start to finish, it is about the simplest process around if someone needs no-hassle digitization done.

Scanmyphotos.com and *scancafe.com* also offer the ability to digitize photos, negatives, slides, video tapes, and motion pictures. Both have generally good reviews, offer lower prices and quicker turnaround, but the overall experience does not seem as polished as legacy box.

If you do not trust sending your materials to an online store, you can try in person at places like CostCo, Walgreens, and CVS. They all offer services like VHS, photo, and slide digitization.

Chapter 7

Tech Instruction

Now that the equipment is set up and you feel confident running through the digitization process, it is time to think about training staff and the public.

You play a crucial role here, not only in teaching these tech skills to those who want to digitize, but also in alleviating any fears they may have about the technology, and giving them the means to preserve their memories and reconnect with the past.

It is important to find clear, simple, and concise ways to convey the information necessary to learn the equipment and related processes. The importance of making it understandable cannot be overstated.

Depending on what equipment and media support you have decided to provide, you will have to determine what is most important to teach. It is a good idea to start small.

By this point, you should have a good idea of what digitization capabilities your community is looking for. Teaching can take a large toll on staff time and resources, so make sure to teach what is most in demand. This will result in more efficient digitization sessions for those who work with the most popular formats, freeing up your staff to help with less popular forms of media and issues that patrons may run into.

WHAT TO TEACH

This may be simple if your lab is set up for one specific process. If you have a scanner, it will be easy to focus on scanning. If you have multiple technologies, try focusing on what is most in demand.

While it may be tempting to teach more niche subjects, make sure you have your main base covered before branching out. It helps to cover the main process in a class, and leave more obscure, or less encountered issues for quick problem solving during the problem itself or for one-on-one appointments.

For example, at AHML our digitization classes are divided into the following:

- Digitize your slides and photos
- Digitize your records and cassettes
- Digitize your VHS tapes and video cassettes
- Digitize your 8mm, Super 8 and 16mm films

For each of these classes, we bring the equipment into our training center, run everyone through the basic terminology, and then through the process for each item.

Naturally, questions arise, and we give time to take care of them. For anything specific to a certain patron or medium, we take care of on a case-by-case basis. The aim of these classes is to familiarize patrons with the process, so they feel more comfortable using the lab on their own time, with their own materials.

WHAT CAN STAFF SUPPORT?

One of the biggest challenges that libraries face in offering more tech-centered services is staffing them. It is important to be realistic about what your staff can support, whether you assign a current employee to the role or if you are looking to hire someone new.

Many libraries recruit anyone on staff who is somewhat comfortable with technology and go from there. Survey staff for interest, gauge their competency level, and work from there to see what level of education and support you can offer.

If someone is more adventurous and up for a challenge, do your best to support learning opportunities, and give them a chance to become the go-to expert in your organization for digitization, whether in general, or for something more specific, like digitizing video, or working with scrapbooks and photos.

HOW IN-DEPTH TO GO

One of things I have found most challenging in teaching people technology is deciding how in-depth to go. Technology can be very complex, but the concepts can be made simple. How much do patrons need to understand? How much do they want to understand? These are questions that are important to address.

It helps to spend a few minutes with an individual to size up his or her knowledge and comfort level with technology. While a large component of digitization is taking advantage of an opportunity to teach someone about technology, we need to be realistic and work within the realm of the patron's own desires, patience, and willingness to learn.

You will encounter patrons who are willing to learn, and want to learn! These are people you can go a bit deeper with. It might be worth going beyond the surface steps required to scan a photo, and let them know about the difference between JPEG and TIFF, and different options for naming their files and storing. This is always beneficial, since this knowledge will help them make better decisions about their digitization projects. Take them as deep as they would like to go and as far as you can take them. They will benefit from more information and make better decisions as a result.

Of course, you will encounter resistance as well. There will be patrons who want you to do it for them (of course, that is not the business we are in), or who want to learn the minimum amount of steps possible to achieve their goal. As long as they are learning the steps themselves, I find it OK to be practical, show them the steps it takes to complete the process, let them know that you can go more in-depth if possible (and help them make more informed decisions), or let them go at their own pace.

These decisions are personal, considering the value of the materials, so it is always good to inform them enough to make wise decisions about how they digitize their materials.

At the very least, you want them to understand the limits of the format they choose, the consequences of file storage, and how to deal with their original materials.

ONE-ON-ONE APPOINTMENTS

One-on-one appointments are often the first method used for teaching the public how to utilize technology. While they can constrain staff resources, they are effective at properly training someone and addressing individual concerns and issues regarding their specific, personal projects.

The main advantages of one-on-one appointments are the personal approach, length of time, and specificity that can be achieved.

By breaking down the education setting to a single teacher and single student, any walls put up in a classroom setting tend to fall away. Student are more likely to ask questions on their mind, without the fear of embarrassment. They feel more at home and more comfortable, leaving them more likely to learn and take away knowledge, and to leave with positive experience.

One-on-ones allow for a set amount of time to accomplish the goals at hand. Not all issues need to or can be resolved in one appointment, so some follow-up sessions may be necessary.

These appointments allow for great specificity as well. Rather than hoping a generic class topic will answer their questions, a one-on-one allows the instructor and student to get to the heart of the matter and to address specific needs.

A few things to keep in mind when setting up one-on-one appointments.

- If you can, have a go-to staff member delegate and assign the appointments. He or she can be the focal point through which all appointments can be funneled, so that requests are fulfilled in order, and to a staff member with the appropriate knowledge.
- Set a time limit. Whether you choose 30 minutes or 60 minutes, it is helpful for both parties to know what they are in for.
- Set expectations. Not only is a time limit helpful, but let them know what can reasonably be addressed by library staff, and what sorts of materials or projects can be digitized.
- Be prepared. Gather information about the desired outcome when the request is made, or with a phone call before so that you can be better prepared. Make sure the patron brings all necessary materials, including a storage device, and the login information for any e-mail or cloud accounts that may be used to store digitized assets.
- If necessary, divide up the materials to be covered over the course of several one-on-one appointments. It is important to set expectations regarding the allotted time, and what can be realistically covered in that period.

Depending on the size of your staff and time resources available, one-on-ones may or may not be the best way to go. If you have service desk staff who will be assisting with digitization projects, appointments may work only if there is more than one person working the desk so that there is someone ready to help the public at all times.

CLASSES

Classes are a great way to introduce larger groups to the digitization opportunities you now have available. By teaching many patrons at once, you can save staff time and get them through the doors quicker and on their way to digitizing their materials.

The main advantage of classes is their ability to help many patrons at once without tying up staff for too long. This is especially helpful if the patrons already have some general tech knowledge. They will be able to learn quickly, get a general sense of the process specific to the media they would like to digitize, and will feel more comfortable getting in the lab and starting on their projects.

Classes also offer students the ability to learn from one another. In my experience, sometimes conversations will pop up during a class, and participants are able to share knowledge, best practices, and sometimes introduce the instructor to something new. This also ties in very well to the community aspect of digitization.

In my own library, and in many others, classes typically range from one to two hours. This is generally a good length of time for covering the basics of a topic, giving ample time for questions, and being able to have a hands-on portion if your resources provide such an opportunity.

It also helps to show participants the actual space they will be using on their own time. This can help relieve any anxiety they may have about coming in to use the space, and will help them feel more comfortable from the get-go.

When teaching, the following are some guidelines to keep in mind for a successful experience for everyone involved.

- Have all your materials ready. This includes your presentation, class guideline, handouts, or other relevant materials.
- Point out the exits and restrooms.
- Go over your cell-phone policy.
- Gauge your classes' experience level and their expectations. It is OK to tailor each class according to your audience.
- Make sure to explain any tech jargon so that everyone is on the same page.
- Defer complex or student-specific questions to the end of class.
- Make sure to stop at regular intervals and make sure everyone is following along and understands things up to that point.
- If the class is hands-on, make sure to walk around and ensure everyone is following along.
- Be prepared to show additional examples or materials if there is extra time. You can also allow for additional questions.
- At the end of class, make sure to plug for other classes that your library offers.
- Mention any relevant databases you may have, such as Lynda.com or Gale Courses.

Classroom

Where will you be teaching classes? A spare room that your library has available? A new space constructed for training and education?

Ideally, your room should be easily accessible and visible. Good visibility encourages passersby to ask about the classes, and observe ones that are currently happening. This all helps to draw residents in even further. It is a great way to engage them with the digitization classes, and any other local history and genealogy opportunities your library might offer.

Class Size

The size of your class may play a factor in the way you teach digitization. Smaller classes offer the opportunity for more personalized assistance, and more hands-on training. Larger classes will push you more to presentations and demonstrations, while still doing your best to offer hands-on time and draw them into the digitization services.

Hands-on training is still very important to provide, even with larger classes. Without the ability to try for themselves, many patrons will not return to use the equipment on their own, even if they know help will be available.

You will find ways to do the best with what you have. Digitization offers challenges for hands-on training, since it is expensive to have as many scanners (or other pieces of equipment) as there are students in the class. Materials are also personal, so not everyone may be comfortable digitizing them in a public space. Having materials for them to digitize helps, as well as giving them time to come up as a group and play around with the equipment. Sometimes it is just the act of seeing the equipment up close that gives them the confidence to return and try it on their own.

Equipment

The equipment you have in the classroom will shape the teaching experience. At the bare minimum, a computer for the instructor and projector will be needed to demonstrate the digitization process. You will also need the digitization equipment, either as a permanent fixture in the classroom, or borrowed from your lab where patrons can work on their digitization projects.

SELF-GUIDED LEARNING

Staff will not always be available for assistance, however some digitizers will want to get started on their own, and prefer to learn on their own. This is where self-guided learning can help.

While many products and software titles have tutorials, it may help to write the guides yourself. You know your community better than anyone, so your own voice can help the self-guided learners more effectively.

Be clear about the steps you are taking, do not leave out small steps, and do not assume your user knows anything in particular. What might seem obvious to you may never cross the mind of someone new to this process. Use simple language, make it understandable, and make it friendly.

On the other hand, you will need to draw the line somewhere. You can go off on a million tangents while writing a guide. In terms of the technical side, this could be exhausting. Do your best to keep the information relevant to the specific process you are outlining, and define only those things necessary for digitization. Give them resources at the end of the guide for further learning, and let the users take that upon themselves if they would like.

Make sure to focus on achieving the specific digitization goal you are outlining. The goal is that a patron can walk in with a digitization need, be able to sit down in your lab, follow the self-guided learning, and walk away with his or her items digitized.

MAKE IT UNDERSTANDABLE

In the previous section, I outlined a few tips for effective self-guided learning. This can and should be carried over to all forms of tech education.

It may seem obvious to make digitization understandable, but with the DIY ethos in mind, it should be the focus. Our patrons come from all walks of life, with varying levels of tech knowledge, so we need to make this process practical, realistic, and helpful.

Language

The language used in guides, one-on-one appointments, and classes should be straightforward, friendly, and simple.

Technical jargon will only make things harder to understand and make it more difficult for the user to make it through the process. If any technical terms are needed, make sure to explain them upfront, and feel free to use a simpler, more approachable word for it.

The language should be simple. There is no need for long-winded explanations. Use common, everyday language, in a way that your patron will understand.

The approach should also be friendly. While digitization is important, this is not the end of the world, nor should our patrons feel any pressure or anxiety about the process. This should be an enjoyable project for everyone.

Stay on Track

Make sure to keep your goal in mind. When teaching any technical topic, it is easy to get sidetracked and end up explaining further than necessary. While we want everyone to learn, we need to walk that fine line of knowledge and learning. We want to give them enough information to go off of, but not so much that they are overwhelmed and give up.

Once the foundations have been laid, any user seeking additional knowledge will find it at his or her own pace, and we can be there to help him or her.

It helps to define terms and concepts that apply directly to the digitization process at hand, but give students the opportunity to learn more by giving them additional resources, and ways to contact you for further learning.

Cover Your Bases

Make sure to outline every step of the process for your user. There is nothing more frustrating than glossing over small steps that are obvious to you, but not to someone learning the process.

Of course, you have to assume something, especially when teaching a class, such as level of tech knowledge. It is sometimes safe to assume basic keyboard, mouse and file management skills, but beyond that, be prepared to explain and assist.

It is a good idea to go through the process yourself several times to make sure you cover all the small details. Ask a few coworkers (preferably with varying levels of experience) to use your instructions as well. This will quickly identify any weak spots in your instructions, and help you gain perspective on how others will perceive the guide.

Remember, your guide will always make sense to you. Your brain will quickly fill in little gaps that might be missing, but these are essential to a first-time user.

Online Guides

If you have already prepared materials for class or for self-guided learning, you can help users in advance by placing them online.

Putting these resources on your website will give users a chance to familiarize themselves ahead of time, and refresh their knowledge.

These guides can simply be PDF version of class handouts or guides that have been placed online for the patron's convenience.

Databases and Other Resources

If creating your own guides and offering staff-taught classes is too much for your library to handle, at least in the beginning, there is nothing wrong with pointing your patrons to resources the library already has to offer.

Point them in the direction of any books you may have on digitization, scanning, editing video, and so forth.

Do you have any databases that might be relevant? Many libraries now offer access to Lynda.com, a service offering thousands of tutorial videos on various software and technologies. Specifically, you will find a vast amount of information on scanning, video editing, Photoshop, and other titles and technologies very relevant to digitization. Anyone who is serious about learning will find a wealth of knowledge here.

Chapter 8

Programs, Display, and Access

With so much of our community's history now digitized, how can we take advantage of their convenience to share our stories and connect with our own community even further? This section will provide an overview of various methods for creating programs, displays, and other ideas for connecting with local history and community stories.

Once some of your patrons have completed their digitization projects, some of them may want to take their collection to the next level, and share it with the community. Other patrons may not even know about your digitization services, and you may be wondering how to better engage the community.

Programs give you the opportunity to take this local history to the public, and give your residents the chance to connect and share their memories with others.

Displays offer more passive ways to showcase digitized materials, always keeping local history in the minds of those who use the library.

Providing access falls right in line with the libraries' mission. Not only do we provide access to information, but to the history of our communities and those who inhabit them.

From digitization clubs and meet-ups to community specific displays of history, and online galleries, related programs and displays are an important step in the digitization process.

PROGRAM IDEAS

While there is no limit to what sorts of programs you can offer, I will outline a few ideas to get the wheels turning. Since it covers a range of topics—from technical to storytelling—the possibilities for related programs run the gamut.

Themed Programs

Our histories and the documents that make them up span far and wide. We come from varying backgrounds, countries, cultures, and institutions. The programs and displays we put together should honor that diversity, and focus on certain areas when it makes sense.

Choosing a theme for your program will help clarify the people you are seeking out for digitization. Being specific is also educational, and your community may be exposed to a culture or niche community they were not knowledgeable of.

Themes can focus on specific ethnic or cultural groups, even subgroups within any certain community. They can also celebrate a specific day or event in your community's history. Particular buildings, places, or religious grounds may also prove to be a worthwhile focus for your program. Every community is different, so the themes available will be unique to yours. I encourage you to seek out new and interesting ways to focus your local history efforts and to engage and connect the community with your area's special history.

Digitization Clubs

Consider connecting patrons not only after digitization is complete, but also for the process itself. The sense of community, empowerment, and support is something that patrons will benefit greatly from while learning a new skill.

Getting people together to learn the process can be a great complement to, or replacement for classes, depending on your staffing capabilities.

If there are groups of friends who want to learn the process together, there is a better chance they will get more out of it, and enjoy it more since they are spending time with people who they already have a rapport with.

While not specific to digitization, this is something we have begun to offer at AHML, and we refer to it as Tech a la Carte. Groups of friends or employees can request a class on something specific, and we will prepare a session for the group so they can learn together in a comfortable environment.

With a process like digitization, that entails tech, project management, and storytelling skills, learning with a group or with friends may be the draw that brings residents in to your services.

With a club, you can teach them not only the technical side, but also bring in guest speakers, or those from your genealogy department to round out the whole experience.

Oral History

While many of the program ideas regarding genealogy and local history revolve around our digitized physical materials, we should not forget about oral history. The power of the human voice and storytelling is a key component in connecting with our history.

As with digitization programs, oral history is also enjoying increased popularity. With programs like StoryCorps (in conjunction with ALA and the Institute of Museum and Library Services), especially their recent StoryCorps @ Your Library program, there are many resources available for starting or hosting oral history programs and events.

Just this year, StoryCorps @ Your Library selected 10 libraries (out of many more that applied) to use its model of preserving local voices to further engage its communities by providing guidelines, equipment, training, and more. We can look to programs like these to put together our own programs.

Each participant receives a copy of their interview, and with permission, the library retains a copy. The recording is also contributed to the collection at the American Folklife Center at the Library of Congress (StoryCorps, 2015).

With some basic equipment, like a USB microphone, or handheld digital recorder, and a computer, some free software like Audacity, working oral histories into your local history collection is a great way to round out your services.

DISPLAY

Programs are great for bringing people together and interactively engaging them with local history, but providing displays offers more time accessible ways to connect with a larger audience.

Displays also provide a great background to the everyday experience at the library, and offer more serendipitous interactions.

In-House Exhibits

Providing materials for display in your library is a simple way to begin engaging the community with local history. Just like with programs, displays can be themed and cover a specific community or event, or any other focus that might be of interest to your residents.

There are a variety of ways to provide displays. Some of the most straightforward involve the type you have regularly seen in libraries. Either on a wall or in display case, you will find photos, documents, or posters on display. These can either be simply the digitized copy of a photo or document or something more thought out, such as a timeline graphic made in Photoshop.

Of course, we can take advantage of the tools we have and display something a bit more engaging and dynamic. If your library has digital signage, or even a computer monitor or TV available, displaying videos, slideshows, or interactive displays is an option.

Even with technologies such as virtual reality (think Oculus Rift), you can find ways to make the history shine from multiple mediums.

Online Exhibits

It is a great time to connect with our communities and share our stories online. One of the easiest ways to share your local history with the community is through online means. It is affordable, accessible, and open for everyone.

One online exhibit is on display through AHML. Founded in 1887, Arlington Heights celebrated its Quasquicentennial, or 125th anniversary in 2012. As a gift to the community, the Arlington Heights Memorial Library decided to build an online exhibit, of local history memorabilia.

This website, entitled Home Sweet Home, is an online pinboard that allows residents to upload photos, audio, and video for everyone to see. It has a similar layout and feel to Pinterest, but with a look all its own, and was developed in-house.

Users can sign up with a simple username and password, and from their account can upload any of their materials, categorize them, and even comment on memories that other people have uploaded.

An online gallery can also be more straightforward, such as a simple webpage on your library's website, providing access to photos, videos, and audio that patrons would like to share.

Popular sites that offer the ability to display your photos include Flickr, Tumblr, Facebook, Instagram, Dropbox, Google Photos, and iCloud.

Sharing with Friends and Family

For many, while sharing with the community is a great pleasure, they will want to share with those who are closest to them, friends and family. Just as with online displays for the community, there are easy and convenient methods for sharing collections with loved ones.

ACCESS

This brings us to our next section, Access, since at this point, not only are we trying to provide displays of content, but also make sure that it is accessible to everyone.

It is important that the content intended for the public is easily accessible, and not limited to formats that only certain people have the power to access. And for this who are looking for a more exclusive (think family and friends) experience, it is important to be able to control access to materials.

Sharing Digitized Materials Online

There is a good chance that many people will want to share their content online once their projects are finished. Sharing their history is one of the main reasons patrons will come to use your library's equipment.

Back in the chapter on storage, we discussed several methods for backing up our data to the cloud. Some of these services, such as Dropbox, Google Drive, and iCloud, offer sharing and display abilities as well.

With options like Facebook, Twitter, Tumblr, Flickr, and more, it is easy to get started with sharing your story. However, there are a few things you will want to keep in mind before posting materials online.

All of these services offer the ability to control who can see your photos, video, or hear your audio. Facebook, for example, allows you to share photos only with those who are your friends. Dropbox allows you to share folders of photos with other specific Dropbox users, or by sharing a link, which can be reached only by those with the link.

Who Owns My Photos?

This may seem obvious. You own it, of course. But it is not always that simple though when using many of these social media services. When you make an account on any of these sites, you are agreeing to their individual terms of service. It all depends on what you or the patron is comfortable with personally, but it is worth understanding the ins and outs of these agreements.

While there have been many circulating articles and rumors claiming that some of these major sites own your photos, this is generally not true. They often retain the right, once you agree to their terms, to use your photos for internal promotion, say to market a campaign to other users of the site. It is important to carefully read each site's individual terms of use before sharing your photos.

Who Can See My Photos?

Again, each social network has its own individual settings when it comes to these options. Many sites, including Facebook, allow you to control who sees your photos. You can often choose between friends, friends of friends, everyone, or to keep all content private.

If privacy is the main concern, a social network such as Facebook or Flickr may not be the best option for you. Services like Dropbox allow you to house photos privately in your cloud account, and send links only to those people you choose, password protected if you want, to a specific photo album or file.

What If I Want Other People to Use My Photos?

If you want to share, you can! For example, Dropbox allows your files to be downloaded, so that those you grant permission to, can retain their own copies. Flickr allows this as well.

Other sites, like Facebook and Instagram, are focused on displaying photos, and do not offer a convenient way of downloading other people's images.

The easiest way to grant others permission to reuse your materials is to license them under Creative Commons.

Creative Commons is a nonprofit organization that provides a standardized way to give the public permission to use your content. The user can choose the conditions of use.

For example, its least restrictive license, _Attribution CC BY,_ lets others "distribute, remix, tweak, and build upon your work, even commercially, as long as they credit you for the original creation."

Its most restrictive license, _Attribution-NonCommercial-NoDerivs CC BY-NC-ND,_ only allows the public to "download your works and share them with others as long as they credit you, but they cannot change them in any way or use them commercially."

Creative Commons is not a replacement for copyright, but works alongside it. If you are interested in licensing anything under the Creative Commons system, you can find more information at creativecommons.org.

ACCESSIBLE FORMATS

Since equal access is important for our institutions, it is best to choose formats that are easily accessible. Luckily, most of the formats discussed earlier in this book are widely accessible.

The catch is—you make the assumption that viewers have a computer and Internet access. While this is very common, and your library likely offers both, this is where offering physical displays can ensure accessibility to everyone.

If you choose an online method for display, major players like Flickr and Dropbox use web standards to ensure accessibility to a wide range of people. If you end up going the proprietary route, or making your own webpage for displays, make sure to keep files small for quick loading times, design an intuitive navigation, and adhere to web standards for maximum accessibility.

JPEGs are the most accessible photo format. MP3 and WAV files will play on most computers. Video does not have a clear winner, but MOV will play on any Mac, AVI, an older format, plays on any PC, and h.264 and MP4 are common formats right now.

Chapter 9

The Future of Digitization

It is always important to look ahead and see what advances are in store. Having a grasp of upcoming changes and improvements to digitization can help us better handle future issues, and provide new, relevant, and helpful services and technologies to our patrons.

The future of digitization will not necessarily only involve new hardware technologies for digitizing materials we have. It will also likely involve converting from current digital formats to other formats just as we have done in the past.

ACCESSIBILITY

As mentioned earlier, digitization does not only require going from analog to digital, but in converting digital objects to different digital formats for keeping up with changing technologies and changing times.

These days, many people are getting their media through streaming services over the Internet. Think about your favorite DVD. Where are you going to play them in 10 years? You might not have a working player, and even, if you went to the store to look for one, it might be hard to find. If you do find one, it will probably be an expensive purchase.

Dilemmas like these make it necessary to look ahead at the future. At the moment, if you have important files on DVDs, it is probably time to start looking into moving or copying them to another, more relevant and modern format.

This does not mean the DVD is irrelevant at this point. Still, a DVD may outlast other newer technologies, but it might not be easily accessed. This is another reason why it is important to have multiple copies in multiple formats.

Other future digitization technologies most likely include better organizational strategies and systems for accessing and arranging all of your digitized materials on organizational level and on a personal level. Will also probably see more reliable storage, more intuitive data redundancy solutions, and easier ways to access your files anytime. Even today with ubiquitous cloud syncing on our smartphones, there is a good chance you are able to access your photos anywhere, or use convenient services like Google Drive or iCloud.

3D SCANNING AND PRINTING

Libraries are no longer a stranger to three dimensional (3D) printing. Over the past few years, many institutions, both public and private, have developed their own 3D printing programs, some equipped with classes and support for designing objects.

But what about digitizing 3D objects? Photos, sounds, motion pictures, letters. These are all great things to have, holding in them the voices of loved ones and ancestors, and the imagery of times past.

But what about that pendant that has been handed down for generations. What if we could digitize it? That is what 3D scanning can begin to offer us.

For example, the Smithsonian launched Smithsonian X 3D, a lab dedicated to digitizing items in their vast collection. Currently, they have a goal of digitizing a specific 10 percent of the collection, moving on to larger amounts as technology progresses (Waibel, 2015).

3D scanning offers not only the ability to capture an object's physical shape, but to track its condition and changes over time, as well as offering the public the ability to interact with the majority of collections that are not on display at any given time.

They currently offer the ability to browse a section of 3D scans, or models, in their collection at http://3d.si.edu/browser.

Naturally, 3D printing, coupled with 3D scanning, could allow patrons to engage with their families or local history in a new and deeper way. Imagine digitizing and printing copies of objects handed down for generations, or, potentially enhancing, or making corrections or changes to these objects as well.

These technologies are in their infancy, but will no doubt prove to be a great addition to the digitization services offered by libraries.

STORAGE IMPROVEMENTS

Since the first hard drives developed in the 1950s, storage has consistently become more affordable, more abundant, and more reliable, and that trend shows no signs of slowing.

Hard drives, as we know it, will probably still be around for some time, although with new technologies. With techniques like longitudinal recording, we are looking at the ability to store more data in a smaller space, and with heat-assisted magnetic recording, there are predictions of storing up to 6.25TB on just 1 square inch of surface area.

SSDs, the faster, less-prone-to-mechanical-failure hard drives mentioned earlier, will continue to drop in price, see speed increases, and have better storage capacities. They will also see smarter storage algorithms, increasing the drive's lifespan (since an SSD has a limited number of times data can be read or written before it wears out).

The next generation of optical storage media, such as DVDs and Blu-Rays, are being developed. GE, for example, is working on holographic storage, using the same form factor as DVDs, and aims to be cheap and abundant like previous disc-based media. Sizes are being predicted up to 1TB per disc. These discs will also offer a lifespan of 30 years (Herrman, 2010).

Other improvements seem farther out, but are nonetheless being actively explored. One method is using DNA and biological material to store data. This could be especially useful since DNA is very stable (tens of thousands of years), can always be read (unlike other formats where technology becomes obsolete and hard to find), and is readily available (Carrol, 2013).

Other methods include molecular memory storage, using individual molecules to store data, and even using quantum computing to perform data storage (Plafke, 2013).

MOBILE DIGITIZATION

In some ways, mobile digitization is having a moment. As mentioned earlier, digitization is not only the transformation of analog content to digital, but also directly digitizing our world in photos, video, and audio.

With the proliferation of smartphones, tablets, and digital cameras, so much of the content we see and hear has been created on mobile devices. Things will only likely continue in this direction. Being able to so conveniently capture and share moments of our lives at any place or moment has opened up new possibilities for documentation.

This also brings up issues of quality and organization. One could argue that much of this direct digitization results in digital noise, or an abundance of content that does not add much value to our lives. But there are still times when having the ability to capture a moment helps us to share important events with those we love, and save them for generations.

Mobile cameras have also played a role in analog to digital digitization. There are a number of apps one can get for their smartphones that let them quickly "scan" real-world documents and photos. While these are not archive quality reproductions, they help us to make quick access copies of things on the go.

They also include functions like optical character recognition. For example, some apps allow you to take photos of business cards, then recognize the text and organize the name, business, and phone number into a convenient digital format, or may add the information into a new contact.

Chapter 10

Review

Let us take a look back at everything covered so far. There is a lot to keep in mind when starting a DIY digitization program, so here are the most important things to remember.

THE BASICS

- Digitization usually refers to the conversion of analog materials into a digital format, such as scanning photos or converting videos. In a bigger sense, it also covers the conversion of any data to a digital format, such as taking a photo, or creating digital content in general.
- Digitization is not a replacement for the original. Remember to consider why you are digitizing any given material. Do you need access copies? Are you looking to fix blemishes and other issues with your material? Maybe you want to ensure you have safe, secure, and redundant copies. Whatever the reason is, relying solely on a digital copy may come back to haunt you. If you must discard an original, make sure to think it through.
- The first major digitization projects were done by universities and museums starting in the 1970s, but grew larger and more accessible through the proliferation of consumer-level computers and scanners in the 1990s.
- Today, digitization is widely accessible with powerful and affordable computers, and other hardware made specifically for converting analog formats into the digital realm. This includes scanners, A/D converters, software, and even our mobile devices.
- Digitization refers to the process of conversion, whereas digital preservation is what we do with those materials to preserve them.
- Reasons to digitize include preservation, personal connection, further study, enhancement, and community building.
- Offering digitization services benefits residents the most when it is made accessible, simple, and meaningful.
- The key to any successful digitization project is to properly prepare by organizing materials, cleaning your environment, and assessing the scope of your project.

GETTING STARTED

- Make your case for the program by garnering support from library administration. Stress the benefits, such as local history engagement, tech education, staff growth opportunities, and community building.
- Seek out funding through a variety of sources, including the general budget, grants, book sales, Friends of the Library, or by partnering with other community institutions.
- Plan out how you will staff the digitization program. Consider using current staff who are interested in and/or skilled with technology and genealogy. If your budget allows, look into hiring someone new, potentially from outside of the library world who possesses the necessary tech skills. Lastly, utilize volunteers to staff your new service.
- Assess the community's needs by keeping an ear to the ground for particular requests or formats that residents are looking to digitize. Focus your initial service on the most popular needs of the community.
- Think about how much support you can offer. Be realistic and set expectations when beginning to work with residents. Support what you can, offer resources for further learning, and encourage residents to take the process into their own hands and support them.
- Consider the space you will place the equipment in. An empty office or other room may work, or a new space may be an option if there is funding and/or a renovation planned. Weigh the benefits of a public space or private space, and plan accordingly, based on the type of community you are serving.
- Begin to look into the hardware and software you will need, dependant on your community's needs, the space you have, and the budget you can work with.

WHAT TO DIGITIZE

- There is a wide range of materials that residents can digitize, ranging from photos and documents to physical objects and motion pictures.
- Work with residents to determine what is worth digitizing to them, and consider what materials might be particularly valuable to your library's local history collection, or to any other program you may be considering.
- Do not forget modern forms of materials worth saving or archiving, such as websites, blog posts, tweets, and other items.

THE EQUIPMENT

- Scanners, used to digitize slides, photos, and other documents, are usually the first piece of hardware opted for in a digitization program. Flatbeds are the most common, offering an accessible price point and easy operation. Specialty scanners offer focused features on specific formats, such as slides or film negatives. Bulk scanners offer the benefit of quick, sweeping scans of large amounts of materials, but sometimes at the cost of quality. Book scanners offer the ability to scan bound materials. Lastly, there are DIY methods for creating your own scanners, such as a bulk slide scanner and book scanner.

- For audio and video, analog to digital converters, or A/D converters, do the digitization. These are either standalone units that connect to a computer via Fire-Wire, USB, or Thunderbolt, or are built into certain playback units themselves, such as a cassette deck with a USB connection.
- Digitizing motion pictures presents more of a challenge than other formats, since reliable playback units are hard to come by, and film is sometimes in poor condition. Professional digitization units start at around $4,000, which is often more than many libraries can afford. DIY methods, such as recording a projected image off a wall, are suitable for access copies and for viewing.
- The computers you get for your lab will be dependent on what your IT staff suggests, and the software you will be using for digitization.
- The software you use will likely be the software that comes with your equipment, but there are many good, third-party options available. Other software worth considering focuses on editing and restoration of digitized materials, such as Photoshop or Audacity.
- You will want to store your data in multiple places, ideally somewhere other than your computer's primary hard drive. Options include external hard drives, flash drives, and cloud storage.
- Make sure your storage device is formatted correctly. NTFS works best for Windows, HFS+ for Mac, and exFAT for drives needed to work on both platforms. FAT32 works as well, but only with files under 4GB.

USING THE GEAR

- Prepare for your project before you begin digitizing. Make sure to organize your materials, and have a clear goal in mind. Set up your equipment and test it to verify everything is in working order before beginning. If any of your materials are damaged, dirty, or flawed, do your best to clean or restore them beforehand. Make sure to seek professional help if you are unsure of how to properly clean old materials.
- Determine what sort of copies you are going to be making. Access copies are lower quality, easier to access version of your media, while preservation copies are high-quality reproduction, meant for long-term storage and archiving.
- Ensure your space is clean and ready for digitization. Make sure it is well ventilated, has ample space for working, is away from windows, and is properly equipped with network access, and enough power for all the gear.
- For scanning, you are going to want to determine the specific settings to digitize at. Remember, DPI is the resolution, or quality and detail you will scan at, starting at 300 DPI, which scans at a photo's native size. JPEGs are great as good quality, yet lightweight files for e-mailing, the web, and smaller prints. TIFFs are higher-quality, higher-file size photos, great as archived versions and high-quality prints.
- For video, you are probably going to digitize in an all-in-one VHS to DVD unit, or using a hardware interface that connects a video playback device to the computer, which then uses software to convert the video. Make sure to use a format that suits your compatibility and file size needs. Common formats include MPEG, MOV, and MP4. Remember that digitization happens in real time, and additional

time is needed whenever converting to a different format on a computer. Transfer times are also long, but can be reduced using a fast connection such as USB 3.0 and Thunderbolt.

- Audio is similar to video, in that it requires real-time conversion, uses similar hardware, but does not need as much conversion time in the digital realm. Common formats include WAV, AIFF, MP3, and AAC.
- Motion pictures are the most difficult to process, but options are available. Professional units start around $4,000, but a DIY method may work, such as recording a projected image through a digital camera, or using a telecine box. Make sure to assess the film's condition before proceeding.
- Software can be a great aid in the digitization process. Some programs will be there to digitize the media, such as Epson Scan (scanning), Garageband (audio), or Premiere Pro (video). Other software is great for restoring media, or editing it, like Photoshop and Audacity.

STORAGE, BACKUPS, AND ARCHIVING

- Storage is where your data lives on your computer, usually the machine's primary hard drive. Backups are copies, usually on external hard drives, flash drives, or optical storage, adding a safety net to your data. Archives are long-term storage, also on additional storage devices, but organized and set aside for permanent storage and access.
- Ensure that patrons know how to save their files when digitizing, and what your file storage policy is. Consider using software like Deep Freeze that restores your computer to a default state after each use. Data privacy is an important consideration when setting up your service.
- Keep the 3–2–1 rule in mind when backing up your data. Make at least three copies of your files, in at least two different formats, with at least one stored off-site.
- Hard drives are the main tool for storing data. These can be internal hard drive, or external (usually USB 2.0 or 3.0), or a combination of both for data redundancy. Flash drives provide an affordable and convenient alternative for small amounts of data, as well as CDs and DVDs (although optical storage is not as convenient). Lastly, the cloud provides another safety net for data as a place to create regular backups, accessible from anywhere there is Internet access.
- Consider different physical locations for your backups. Having your data backed up on external hard drives is useful, but having an off-site copy provides protection if your residence is flooded or subject to some other disaster.
- Remember some social media sites may provide additional backup as places your photos, videos, and audio can live, assuming you are comfortable with putting these materials in public. This is not a true backup method, but something to keep in mind as another place your data can reside.
- Name your files appropriately, using proper numbering schemes, relevant names, and consistency to ensure easy access and organization.
- Keep in mind the lifespans of different forms of media. This will play a role in what is easily accessible in the future, as well as how long you can reasonably rely on the data's safety. Newer technologies do not necessarily last longer than older ones.

- Make sure to store your materials properly. In general, keep the stored material in cool, dry places with no temperature fluctuations, and away from sunlight, rodents, pests, and the possibility of flooding.

TECH INSTRUCTION

- Determine what your community wants to digitize most and focus your instruction efforts on that. Assess how much your staff can support, in terms of technical support and guidance, set expectations, and let residents know where they can find additional learning resources.
- Consider one-on-one appointments, classes, and self-guided learning as ways to teach your residents the digitization process. One-on-ones offer great help for those with specific needs and projects, while classes are great for on-boarding larger groups of people and getting them acquainted with the process. Self-guided learning is best for those who are willing to take initiative and dive right in.
- Do your best to keep your classes and guides simple and straightforward, particularly with the language used. Explain concepts and terminology in an easy-to-understand fashion, and make the process feel friendly and accessible.
- Make additional resources available to those who want to take their learning to the next step. These can be books, online guides, or web-based courses such as Lynda.com.

PROGRAMS, DISPLAY, AND ACCESS

- Programs are a great way to engage the community with the materials that have been digitized and the history they represent. Consider different focuses, such as specific nationalities, community events, and other themes.
- Starting a digitization club or group can be a good way to get residents to learn and grow together. By learning with each other, people may feel greater confidence and comfort in asking questions and pursuing their projects.
- Displays can be done in-house, out in the community, or even online. Consider using technology to make materials more accessible, engaging, and interactive.
- When posting online, keep in mind the ease of access, the privacy capabilities, and ownership issues. Each person will have different comfort levels with where he or she displays his or her materials.
- Ensure that materials are not only easy to access, but also utilize widely used formats, so that access is as universal as possible.

THE FUTURE OF DIGITIZATION

- Looking to the future, one of the main considerations to make is accessibility. Choose formats that show good promise of future access and compatibility. Stay current with formats to ensure your data makes it onto reliable, relevant, and supported storage mediums.
- 3D scanning and printing will open a new realm of digitization possibilities and capabilities. Libraries have already begun offering both, but at very introductory

levels, and with a focus on printing. As 3D scanning becomes more accurate and reliable, it will offer a great new way to digitize objects. Larger institutions, such as the Smithsonian, have already begun digitizing their collections and offering access to the public.

- Storage technologies will be improving as well, offering great storage capacities, better reliability, and greater affordability. We will see improvements within current technologies and new storage methods as well.
- Mobile trends will continue as a primary driver in data creation and digital content generation. Our smartphones have become our main cameras and will aid us in documenting our current moments and passing them on to friends, family, and our communities.

Bibliography

ADVC110. 2015. ADVC110 | Grass Valley, a Belden Brand (ADVC110 | Grass Valley, a Belden Brand) http://www.grassvalley.com/products/advc110

Archival Formats. 2015. Archival Formats (National Archives and Records Administration) http://www.archives.gov/preservation/formats/

BinderMinder. 2015. BinderMinder (BinderMinder) http://binderminder.com

Carroll, Alex. 2013. DNA: The Future of Digital Storage?—Lifeline Data Centers (Lifeline Data Centers) http://www.lifelinedatacenters.com/data-center/dnas-digital-storage/

Case, Loyd. 2015. All about Video Codecs and Containers (TechHive) http://www.techhive.com/article/213612/all_about_video_codecs_and_containers.html

CC-222MKIV. 2015. Products: Recorder/Player: CD recorder: CC-222MKIV (Product: CC-222MKIV) http://tascam.com/product/cc-222mkiv/

Cloud Storage. 2011. Cloud Storage: Limits of the Cloud (CCSK Guide) https://ccskguide.org/cloud-storage-limits-of-the-cloud/

Colbert, Donovan. 2011. Facing a Data Apocalypse: The Limitations of Digital Storage (TechRepublic) http://www.techrepublic.com/blog/data-center/facing-a-data-apocalypse-the-limitations-of-digital-storage/

Edwards, Jim. 2014. PLANET SELFIE: We're Now Posting a Staggering 1.8 Billion Photos Every Day (Business Insider) http://www.businessinsider.com/were-now-posting-a-staggering-18-billion-photos-to-social-media-every-day-2014-5

Epson Perfection V600. 2015. Epson Perfection V600 Photo Scanner (Product Information) http://www.epson.com/cgi-bin/Store/jsp/Product.do?sku=B11B198011

Epson Perfection V700. 2015. Epson Perfection V700 Photo Scanner (Epson Perfection V700 Photo, Overview) http://www.epson.com/cgi-bin/Store/jsp/Product.do?sku=B11B178011

Fouts, Janet. 2015. Images and Copyrights: Do It Right (Social Media Today) http://www.socialmediatoday.com/social-business/2015-05-14/images-and-copyrights-do-it-right

Henry, Alan. 2015. How Long Will My Hard Drives Really Last? (Lifehacker) http://lifehacker.com/how-long-will-my-hard-drives-really-last-1700405627

Herrman, John. 2010. The Future of Storage (Gizmodo) http://gizmodo.com/5497512/the-future-of-storage

Intensity Shuttle. 2015. Intensity Shuttle for Thunderbolt™ (Blackmagic Design: Intensity) https://www.blackmagicdesign.com/products/intensity

Jacobi, Jon L. 2015. Digitize Your Analog Life (TechHive) http://www.techhive
.com/article/220783/digitize_your_analog_life.html

Johnston, Leslie. 2012. Before You Were Born: We Were Digitizing Texts (Before You
Were Born: We Were Digitizing Texts) http://blogs.loc.gov/digitalpreservation/
2012/12/before-you-were-born-we-were-digitizing-texts/

Markin, Karen M. 2015. Where Should You Keep Your Data? (The Chronicle of
Higher Education) http://chronicle.com/article/Where-Should-You-Keep-Your/
231065/

M-Track. 2015. M-Audio—M-Track (M-Audio—M-Track) http://www.m-audio
.com/products/view/m-track

National Archives. 2015. Storing Family Papers and Photographs (National Archives
and Records Administration) http://www.archives.gov/preservation/family-ar
chives/storing.html

Osterberg, Gayle. 2013. Update on the Twitter Archive at the Library of Congress
(Update on the Twitter Archive at the Library of Congress) http://blogs.loc.gov/
loc/2013/01/update-on-the-twitter-archive-at-the-library-of-congress/

Ozer, Jan. 2009. Streaming 101: The Basics—Codecs, Bandwidth, Data Rate and
Resolution (Streaming 101: The Basics—Codecs, Bandwidth, Data Rate and
Resolution)http://www.streaminglearningcenter.com/articles/streaming-101-the-
basics—codecs-bandwidth-data-rate-and-resolution.html

Plafke, James. 2013. Individual Molecules: Storage Devices of the Future | Extreme-
Tech (ExtremeTech) http://www.extremetech.com/computing/146690-individ
ual-molecules-storage-devices-of-the-future

PowerSlide 5000. 2015. PacificImage Electronics (PacificImage Electronics) http://
www.scanace.com/scan_pd_1.php?id=36

RetroScan. 2015. moviestuff_home (moviestuff_home) http://www.moviestuff.tv/
moviestuff_home.html

ScanSnap SV600. 2015. FUJITSU Image Scanner ScanSnap SV600 (Fujitsu Global)
http://www.fujitsu.com/global/products/computing/peripheral/scanners/
scansnap/sv600/

Sebastian, Anthony. 2013. How Long Do Hard Drives Actually Live For? | Extreme-
Tech (ExtremeTech) http://www.extremetech.com/computing/170748-how-
long-do-hard-drives-actually-live-for

Sieber, Tina. 2012. CDs Are Not Forever: The Truth about CD/DVD Longevity,
"Mold" & "Rot" (MakeUseOf) http://www.makeuseof.com/tag/cds-truth-cdd
vd-longevity-mold-rot/

SINTEF. 2013. "Big Data, for Better or Worse: 90% of World's Data Generated
Over Last Two Years" (ScienceDaily) www.sciencedaily.com/releases/2013/
05/130522085217.htm

SlidesSnap Pro. 2015. What Is a SlideSnap? (SlideSnap Pro World's Fastest Slide
Scanner) http://slidesnappro.com

StoryCorps. 2015. StoryCorps (StoryCorps) https://storycorps.org/your-library/

Student Press Law Center. 2015. When It Comes to Social Media, Some Old-School
Legal Rules May Not Apply (Student Press Law Center) http://www.splc.org/
article/2014/08/when-it-comes-to-social-media-some-old-school-legal-rules-
may-not-apply

Tape 2 PC. 2015. Tape 2 PC™—Cassette Conversion System—ION Audio—Dedicated to Delivering Sound Experiences (Tape 2 PC™—Cassette Conversion System—ION Audio—Dedicated to Delivering Sound Experiences) http://www.ionaudio.com/products/details/tape-2-pc

Toshiba DVR620. 2015. Toshiba DVR620 DVD/VHS Recorder (Black) (Discontinued) (Amazon.com: Electronics) http://www.amazon.com/Toshiba-DVR620-Recorder-Black-Discontinued/dp/B001T6K7G6

TTUSB. 2015. The Easiest Way to Digitize Your Vinyl (TTUSB Turntable with USB Audio Interface) http://www.numark.com/product/ttusb

Waibel, Günter. 2015. About Smithsonian X 3D (About Smithsonian X 3D) http://3d.si.edu/about

Wright, Jazzy. 2014. Nearly 100 Percent of Libraries Offer Tech Training and STEM Programs, Study Finds (District Dispatch) http://www.districtdispatch.org/2014/07/nearly-100-percent-libraries-offer-tech-training-stem-programs-study-finds/

Index

About the Author

Alex Hoffman runs the Studio at the Arlington Heights Memorial Library in suburban Chicago. Here, he helps patrons digitize their materials, learn new tech skills and work on other creative projects. He might also be found trying to cook a decent meal, spending time outside, or scouring Wikipedia for something interesting. For more info, visit ahoffman.info.